THE SPIRIT OF AMERICAN PHILOSOPHY

SUNY Series in Philosophy
ROBERT C. NEVILLE, EDITOR

The Spirit of
American Philosophy

REVISED EDITION

JOHN E. SMITH

State University of New York Press   *Albany*

In Memoriam
Lt. Joseph Robert Smith, Jr. U.S.A.F.
Missing in Action, 1944

First edition published by Oxford University Press
Published by State University of New York Press, Albany
© 1983 State University of New York
All rights reserved
Printed in the United States of America

For information, address State University of New York Press, State University Plaza, Albany, N.Y., 12246

Library of Congress Cataloging in Publication Data
Smith, John Edwin.
 The spirit of American philosophy.

 (SUNY series in philosophy)
 Bibliography: p. 243
 Includes index.
 Contents: Charles S. Peirce—William James—Josiah Royce—John Dewey—[etc.]
 1. Philosophy, American—20th century.
I. Title. II. Series.
B893.S63   982   191   82-5612
ISBN 0-87395-650-8   AACR2
ISBN 0-87365-651-6 (pbk.)

Since this book was written, there appears to be a growing interest both in the approach to philosophy and in some of the ideas represented by the philosophers discussed in it. At the meetings of the Fourth East-West Philosophers' Conference held in Honolulu in the summer of 1964, it was clear that many of the younger philosophers from the Orient are finding new insights and inspiration in the approach to philosophy and especially in the theory of experience to be found in James, Peirce, and Dewey. In cultures where speculative interest in philosophy has predominated, and where at the same time new and demanding social and political problems are emerging, it is understandable that philosophers will seek for an outlook in which such concerns are central. The importance of the social and the ethical in the philosophy of Dewey and James and, especially, the prominent place given by both to the belief that thought should be directed to the solution of particular, concrete problems help to explain the new interest which the younger philosophers from India and the Far East are showing in the development of philosophy in America.

Moreover, some European philosophers are moving in the same direction. The connection, only recently taken seriously, between the radical empiricism of William James and the basic outlook of phenomenology is leading to a new study of James, focusing on his psychology and the theory of pure experience rather than, as in the past, on his pragmatic theory of knowledge and truth. Peirce is also coming in for considered inter-

pretation; his combination of logical studies and the theory of
signs with a comprehensive speculative philosophy is coming
to be regarded as a bridge between critical and speculative
philosophy.

On the British scene, doubts about the future of the linguistic approach to philosophy, plus the impetus given by Wittgenstein's emphasis in the later writings upon returning to
direct experience for a "second look," are leading to a new
concern for experience. There is now more talk than there has
been for some time about having to force language to conform
to experience rather than vice versa. It is likely, as James indeed predicted, that those who initially approached pragmatism in a patronizing way, declaring it to be merely a philosophy of expediency lacking in rigor, will end by claiming to
have discovered its main contentions themselves. If this happens, we shall have to modify the old jest according to which
philosophical ideas of European origin are said to go to
America when they die.

As for the American philosophical situation, it is clear that
we need to regain the boldness and independence of our
classical thinkers. This is a very different matter from merely
repeating their doctrines, although if we did only this it
would not be worse, from an academic standpoint at any rate,
than repeating, as is now generally done, the philosophical
conclusions of Wittgenstein, Russell, and Moore. The main
problem is that in America today philosophy has become so
completely an academic affair, controlled by the philosophies
of language and analysis, that there seems to be little room
for new basic ideas that can be used to control our interpretation of a wide range of experience. The fact is that the
majority of philosophers has neglected history, literature, religion, art, and even science, in their substantive content; in-

sofar as these fields enter at all, they are used merely as fixed and convenient subject matter for philosophical "analysis" leading to what may be called the "philosophy of" enterprises. In the meantime the discussion of more concrete philosophical issues continues under, so to speak, unofficial auspices in the form of "literary criticism" and "intellectual history," to mention but two examples. The unhappy consequence is that trained philosophers are often not discussing basic issues, while historians and literary scholars are attempting to do so, but are forced to proceed in a somewhat amateur fashion. The fact that the questions are being asked at all, however, testifies to the inescapability of the philosophical dimension.

JOHN E. SMITH

New Haven, Connecticut
September, 1965

American philosophical thinking in the past three-quarters of a century has exhibited its own original and unmistakable spirit. The very existence of such a spirit casts grave suspicion upon everything that has been said about America's being a young country with an old and borrowed mentality. One conviction has been at the center of American reflective thought since Emerson, the conviction that ideas have a cutting edge, that they make a difference, as William James liked to put it, and that they forfeit their claim to our attention just to the extent to which their relevance is not evident. It is no exaggeration to say that in American intellectual life irrelevant thinking has always been considered the cardinal sin. The most damning complaint which can be made against a thinker is that he has lost touch with the facts or that his ideas hold forth no possibilities for concrete consequences. In our tradition, thought is never understood as moving in a realm above historical life; it exists instead as an integral part of that life, imparting to it both direction and interpretation. If this concrete way of viewing philosophical thinking has had its shortcomings in an overemphasis upon immediate and narrowly utilitarian goals, it has also had its power by reflecting what is actually believed and done. In time past, many philosophers have written eloquently of the value and importance of philosophy for ordinary life; American thinkers above all others have been distinguished by their willingness to believe in this importance to the point of so focusing their thoughts that the academic problems of philosophers are overshadowed by the urgent problems of men.

The drive to be relevant does not, of course, guarantee that the ideas developed through that impulse will necessarily be valid. But even if we question the sufficiency of usefulness and fruitfulness as criteria of truth, we must not overlook the fact that appeal to them bespeaks a deep and sincere belief in the temporal and historical importance of the human mind and its products. Pragmatism, to be sure, often betrayed the short-sightedness and the flatness of its mundane outlook upon human life. There is a price to be paid for making our thoughts speak to a limited experience and circumstance, the price of being so completely tied to the moment that we lose sight of the perennial or universal elements that bear on all moments. It is as if no philosophy could do full justice to the demands of a particular time and to all time at the same time. In their passion to speak in a way that would answer to the needs of the situations in which they found themselves, Dewey and James, for example, were guilty of oversimplifying things, of neglecting the imponderables in human experience, and of supposing that being "practical" invariably carries its own justification along with it. Consequently, enduring standards were sometimes sacrificed and there was engendered a general sense not only of the relativity of all things but of the futility of attending to anything not subject to control by human will and ingenuity. In any attempt to lay hold of the spirit of American reflective thinking, forgetting these limitations would be folly. They do not, however, destroy the fundamental point which is of as much importance for those viewing us from outside as it is for ourselves: American philosophers have never been satisfied merely to praise ideas or to expound them; they have been animated rather by the desire to see them embodied and provided with whatever power it is within the capacity of the human self to bestow.

A major tragedy for American intellectual life is that critics at home and abroad have avoided deep involvement; they have tended to participate in our thinking from afar and to learn about it at second hand. Perhaps the lingering suspicion that American philosophical thinking is borrowed from the intellectual capital of the Old World has been the principal cause for such an attitude. But it is difficult to understand how one can estimate the novelty and importance of a set of ideas without first having some direct acquaintance with them. The present world situation makes continued isolation inappropriate at the very least, and it could even prove to be disastrous. As a contemporary philosopher has remarked, the United States is still an undiscovered country intellectually; to deal effectively with the situation it is imperative that lines of communication be established. And it is to be hoped that an interpretation of the spirit and basic drift of American philosophical thinking in what has been called its classic period will be a stimulus to further exploration of the basic materials upon which any interpretation must finally rest.

These studies are thematic in the sense that they seek to express various ways in which certain American thinkers have interpreted human life and culture in philosophical form. The endeavor to understand the main contribution of such men as Charles Peirce, William James, Josiah Royce, John Dewey, and A. N. Whitehead, requires that more attention be paid to basic doctrines and their reflection of American convictions than to the internal development of any philosophical system. In this way we shall be engaged in self-understanding. We shall have to wrestle with the problem of arriving at a clear understanding of our basic motives and beliefs. For it would be curious indeed if, in setting forth the spirit of American philosophy for the benefit of others, we should fail to achieve any deepened grasp of ourselves. If it is true, as Locke vividly pointed out, that no man is a good judge in his own case, we shall ultimately have to discover our own selves with the help of outside interpreters. But it seems reasonable to suppose that such interpreters will be of little value unless they take the time and the pains to discover us at first hand and to discuss our philosophical beliefs as seriously as we discuss theirs.

The idea of writing an interpretation of American philosophical thinking over the past seventy-five years first emerged during work on a critical study of a series of essays, *American Philosophers at Work,* edited by Sidney Hook. That study was published in *The Review of Metaphysics,* December, 1957 under the title, "The Course of American Philosophy" and the response to it was so enthusiastic that I at once saw the point of extending the interpretation.

A word about George Santayana may be in order here. I have not discussed him in this study, for it seems to me that despite his presence in the 'golden age' of American philosophy his thought is not representative of the main drift of American thinking. The American mind, as Santayana himself saw, is voluntaristic and not contemplative; it is moral and moralistic rather than aesthetic; it would sooner give up religion altogether than retain it as mere poetry; it will not accept any theory of reality according to which the self is either an appearance or evanescent. The American mind, in short, has been everything but what Santayana was and stood for.

When it comes to intellectual debts, no one can acknowledge all of them. The principal reason is that so many remain hidden from the one who has incurred them. I have profited much from the dialogue which takes place in a large university with students at all stages of development and with colleagues in one's own as well as other fields. I am grateful for all the conversations, both hurried and at leisure, in which ideas have been exchanged and issues worked over. Without such conversation no philosophy is possible. Above all I am truly grateful for the untiring help of my wife who has successfully combined severe criticism with good sense.

John E. Smith

New Haven, Connecticut
November, 1962

PREFACE TO THE REVISED EDITION

This edition represents the text of the original edition of 1963 with some revisions, omissions, and additions. Chapter VI, "Retrospect and Prospect" has been enlarged to include the substance of "A Fifty Year Retrospective in Philosophy" which was presented as part of a symposium held at the University of Delaware in 1979, and subsequently published in the *International Philosophical Quarterly* (Vol. XXI, No. 2, June, 1981). As the title implies, this discussion aims at a critical interpretation of the philosophical scene, especially in America, up to the present. The final chapter, "The New Need for a Recovery of Philosophy" is the Presidential Address which I delivered at the annual meeting of the American Philosophical Association, Eastern Division, held in Philadelphia in December, 1981. It is my hope that readers will be led to reconsider what I earlier described as "the spirit of American philosophy" in the light of the course that philosophy eventually took under the influence of the reflexive and linguistic turns.

I wish to express thanks to my wife, Marilyn, who teaches philosophy at the University of Hartford, for invaluable assistance both in substance and style, and to Professor Robert C. Neville, a former student of mine and now Professor of Philosophy at SUNY, Stony Brook, for his interest in making the present edition possible. I am grateful as well to Patricia Slatter who has faithfully typed the additions to the text.

JOHN E. SMITH

New Haven, Connecticut
January, 1982

CONTENTS

THE SPIRIT OF AMERICAN PHILOSOPHY

I

Charles S. Peirce: MEANING, BELIEF, AND

LOVE IN AN EVOLVING UNIVERSE

Philosophical thinking in America has provided many surprises and it has rarely followed orthodox patterns in its development. Consequently we should not be astonished to discover that the man largely responsible for initiating America's pragmatic philosophy, with its emphasis upon action and immediate issues, should have been a man of theoretical science, a logician, and a speculative philosopher whom his contemporaries found difficult to understand. Charles Peirce was, and to a degree still is, an enigma. That he was a genuine philosopher, and one of high order, cannot be doubted by anyone acquainted with his thought. But the main drift of his thinking often escapes us and we are still bewildered by the inconsistencies both in idea and expression to be found in his widely diversified works.

Peirce is unique among the so-called classical American philosophers in that he did not hold an academic post. Whether his failure to be connected with a university was a matter of deliberate choice or one of necessity is not so important as the fact itself. Though he was cruelly hedged in by circumstances, both economic and social, Peirce was a free spirit in every sense. No subject was alien to his interest and

3

he did not shrink from seeking relations between parts of the world which most people had long since decided have nothing to do with each other. This accounts for his tendency to talk about God in papers devoted to the philosophy of science and to introduce the theory of hypothetical reasoning when writing about the philosophy of religion. He had a passion for finding things out, for seeing how they work and what they actually show themselves to be; he had little patience with anyone who had decided prior to experience that things *must* be this way or that. Peirce was a genuine empiricist.

Though he was early introduced to mathematics by his father Benjamin Peirce, and was imbued with the spirit of the laboratory and the procedures of the natural sciences, Peirce had an asset which men of science have often lacked. He had a cosmological and metaphysical framework within which to interpret the scope and depth of scientific knowledge. It is not often that one finds in the modern world a mind which is equally at home with the theory of probability and the issues discussed by the schoolmen in the days of Abelard and Thomas Aquinas. Peirce had such a mind, and its rarity contributes to the seeming strangeness of his thought. We are more at home with thinkers whom we can place neatly in fixed categories; pioneers who do not obey the rules invented by us for the purpose of avoiding new ideas and hard problems are usually puzzling to us. But Peirce refused to follow conventional patterns; he was as interested in God as in prime numbers and as much concerned to estimate the cosmic significance of the theory of evolution as to find a solution to the problem of universals.

It is fairly clear that Peirce's straitened circumstances, which forced him to carry an enormous load of extraneous book reviewing and writing of articles in order to make ends meet, were crucial in determining the fragmentary character of his thought. He planned many projects which were never completed, and he failed to develop a consistent view on many issues. It would, however, be an error to suppose that he developed no clear doctrine whatever, and, in fact, if we consider the whole range of his thought there emerges a unity which is as remarkable as it is unexpected.

His pragmatism — or pragmaticism, as he preferred to call it — is absolutely basic to his philosophy, and the doctrines which go to make it up will be found throughout his writings. He did not regard his practicalism in thought as in any way incompatible with his speculative cosmology because, though he believed that thought must find its realization in the act, he was no less convinced that all conduct, including that of the most immediately focused thinking, has implications about the ultimate constitution of the universe. The protracted discussion about a conflict in Peirce's thought between naturalism and transcendentalism points not so much to an ultimate opposition as to a dialectical attempt to combine the concern for factual existence that goes with the outlook of natural science with the unified picture of things that accompanies a rationalism of a Hegel or a Kant. Peirce was both a man of science and a man of wisdom. Who shall say that we do not need both? Who will deny that there are untold advantages in having them together in one man?

Without proposing to sum up Peirce's voluminous writings in a simple formula, we can, nevertheless, gain an insight into his thought by concentrating on his pragmaticism. These ideas were not only basic to Peirce but they also represent that part of his work which had an immediate impact on his contemporaries. James had a good deal to do with establishing the belief that Peirce was the father of pragmatism, and, although Peirce often said that he had picked up certain key ideas from others, the fact remains that he gave expression to the main principles of pragmatism long before the end of the last century. That he stimulated James to develop his own humanistic version of the doctrine is clear enough. If we can understand Peirce's views about *meaning* and about *belief* we shall be in a position to grasp the core of his pragmaticism. With that in hand it will be possible to go further and set forth the main outlines of his cosmic metaphysic — the idea of love or, as he called it, *agapasticism.**

One of the peculiarities of philosophy is that it asks questions about its own questions. Whenever we think about anything at all, we find ourselves *meaning* something, trying to express something. In all of our speaking and writing we take this fact for granted. Philosophical reflection turns back on the process and asks for the meaning of meaning itself. What is it to mean? Do words mean, or ideas, or both, and how? These are the rudimentary questions serving to start the inquiry. It is no secret that philosophers have been exercised over the problem of meaning, perhaps too much so, ever since the time of Descartes. Peirce was very much opposed to the Cartesian solution and his own position was developed, in the beginning at least, in conscious resistance to the rationalist theory of this celebrated seventeenth-century thinker.

Two main features characterize the Cartesian position. First, Descartes thought of the human mind as a power of grasping the meaning of a concept in a wholly intuitive way; secondly, he regarded the mind as self-contained in the sense that its

---

* Words had great attraction for Peirce and he was fond of coining strange terms in order to express his meaning precisely. Sometimes, however, his terminology became clumsy and even confusing. For example, he used the term "agapasm" to mean a mode of evolution brought about by creative love. For the doctrine illustrated in this mode he used the term "agapasticism," and for the weaker thesis that the law of love operates in the universe he used the term "agapism." While all three terms have to do with the same general idea, they cannot be taken as synonyms.

peculiar circumstances — that it belongs to this person, or that it operates in this place at a certain time — do not in any way affect its operation. The mind has, moreover, a purely theoretical thrust; it aims at pure insight and theoretical truth and it has within itself complete autonomy with regard to believing or withholding assent. Descartes carried over into his philosophical reflections the outlook of a mathematician. It seemed to him that clarity of meaning — understanding, for example, the meaning of a circle — is achieved when we apprehend the meaning of certain simple or primitive ideas from which our complex ideas are made up. In the case of the circle we understand what a circle is when we grasp directly the meaning of such concepts as point, center, equidistance, and so on. The gaining of clarity and the avoidance of error involve both the grasping of essential characteristics — what a thing is — and the ability to distinguish it from other things which it is not. The famous criteria of "clear and distinct" set forth in Descartes's *Discourse on Method* were intended to emphasize both aspects. We understand clearly what a thing is when we know its essential characteristics, and we understand these characteristics when we are able to distinguish them, and through them the thing itself, from everything else in the universe.

Descartes believed that the human mind is a wholly theoretical instrument, that it is capable of operating out of context, and that it can apprehend the naked character of things independently of the desires and interests of the self who owns it. Allied with this belief is the further belief that meaning is a *wholly intuitive affair,* that we just "grasp" meanings without the aid of language or other symbolic devices and that we can arrive at clear meanings simply by taking thought and without referring to the behavior of things. Peirce, though he had his own high estimate of the power of reason as mani-

fested in logic and mathematics, raised objections to both of
the Cartesian beliefs. He did not believe that our minds can
function apart from our own selves, our interests and our
plans, and he did not accept the view that thinking takes place
in a vacuum or that it has nothing to do with the circumstances giving rise to reflective thought. In addition, he had
doubts about our power to grasp meanings *intuitively* without
dependence upon language and signs. Peirce's pragmatic
theory of meaning was directed against Descartes's reliance
upon immediacy as the sure road to clarity, and his theory of
belief was directed against the Cartesian view that reason
operates in a vacuum.

The key to understanding Peirce's theory of meaning is
found when we see that it is essentially empiricism with some
subtle and novel twists. Although Peirce criticized the narrow-
ness of traditional empiricism, he was ready to maintain that
our idea of anything is the idea of the sensible effects which
it manifests. The term "effects" in this statement is the central
one. It points to the *behavior* of the object in question, to the
ways in which it will respond when set in relation to other
things and especially when it is manipulated in certain pre-
determined ways designed for the purpose of testing its properties. Instead of regarding the properties of things as inert
qualities possessed by them in an essentially timeless way,
Peirce wanted to interpret them as effects of interactions. In
this way he was attempting to include within the meaning of
an idea the operations or manipulations which go on in the
process of inquiry and testing. The connection later pointed
out between the pragmatic theory of meaning and the operational theory, which states that the meaning of a concept is
identical with a set of laboratory operations, is based on the
fact that both connect meaning with the manipulation of
things in actual measurement or testing. In Peirce's classic
example, when we say that something is *hard* and want to be

clear about our meaning we must think at once of the behavior of the thing. If something is *hard*, there are many things that will not scratch it. When we contemplate the characteristic *hard* we are to understand that its clear meaning consists in the sensible effects which a *hard* substance will exhibit when it is actually put to the test. *Hard*, that is, means the actual fact of scratching or not being scratched when we come to the operation of trying out the case.

We can detect the drift of Peirce's view at once; meaning is being removed from exclusive residence in the "mind" and is now identified with events in the world, including actions which the individual himself may perform. Instead of intuiting directly certain properties or characteristics of things, we are to direct our attention outward to actions and reactions in the physical world, to a series of operations which we can perform for the purpose of seeing how the object in question will behave. The meaning of an idea expressing a property of something will be found in the effects it reveals when we carry out tests. We are no longer to think of a property as something whose meaning we understand by an intellectual grasping quite apart from any tests we might perform to discover the presence of that property. We are asked instead to think of the meaning as including the operation of testing itself; when the test is performed and the sensible effects recorded, those effects *are* the meaning of the idea in question.

Objections to this position were not long in coming, nor was Peirce at a loss for replies. But before one can understand either the objections or the replies it is necessary to expand Peirce's argument and at the same time introduce his doctrine of belief. For at the root of all Peirce's conclusions about logic was his general view of the nature and function of thought. The idea that thought is bound up with belief and that belief, in turn, is connected with action runs throughout the literature of pragmatism. Much has been heard about the central place given to practice in pragmatism and many, both friends and foes, have tried to sum up the position in this one idea alone. The meaning of practice, the ambiguities of the term "practical," and the connection between belief and action are all topics which need to be made much plainer than has been the case in the past.

We have seen Peirce's attempt to reinterpret the meaning of meaning and to direct attention away from immediate apprehensions of the mind and toward the sensible effects produced by the behavior of objects in the physical world. But if we said no more than this, we would not have pointed to anything distinctive or novel such as could justify the claim of the pragmatists to be setting forth a unique philosophical outlook. Old-fashioned empiricism also attacked the rationalist position as represented by Descartes; it too claimed that clarity in our ideas could be achieved only by attending to particular sensible things. True, Peirce and others had modified this view by insisting that the sensible qualities of things be understood as dynamic behavior and not as static and timeless qualities, but this shift itself (Mill had gone this far and he is not generally regarded as a pragmatist) would not suffice to establish pragmatism as a doctrine distinctive in its own right. To do that we need to bring in the crucial idea of the necessary connection between a concept, a belief, and an action.

In one formulation of his doctrine of meaning, one which has caused much discussion over the years, Peirce said:

> Consider what effects, which might conceivably have practical bearings, we conceive the object of our conception to have. Then, our conception of these effects is the whole of our conception of the object.*

* *Collected Papers of Charles Sanders Peirce*, eds. Charles Hartshorne and Paul Weiss, Cambridge, 1935. Vol. 5, p. 402.

Now insofar as this statement means no more than what Peirce had claimed on other occasions, namely, that the idea of something is the idea of its sensible effects, we are still at one with empiricism. But there is a qualifying clause in the statement and it expresses the idea which makes all the difference. We are asked to attend to effects "which might conceivably have practical bearings," and it is imperative that we discover what Peirce meant by the "practical bearings." We must go back to his theory of the function of thought for the answer.

It is important to notice that the thought of the seventeenth and eighteenth centuries was, on the whole, dominated by an ideal of theoretical knowledge. The human self was conceived, by the empiricists and the rationalists alike, as essentially a spectator, and it was taken for granted that the human mind could be understood as an instrument concerned solely with the acquisition of theoretical knowledge. Peirce and the pragmatic empiricists who followed him did not accept this view; their failure to do so was decisive both for their own views and for the arguments of their critics. Peirce started with the conception of man as a being capable of thinking; he started with the concrete individual and with the fact that thinking is always localized and called for on specific occasions within the life span of the self. The *why, where, when,* and *how* of thinking become essential; thought comes to be understood in terms of its purpose in the life of the thinker himself. The mind is no longer a timeless spectator and its function in thinking is no longer taken as the disinterested pursuit of truth. Thought becomes instead the means of producing *belief,* something which is both more and less than knowledge. There is some skepticism in this view, but also considerable power because belief must lead to action. Without action, belief is hollow and dead.

The chief and identifying function of thought is to produce

belief. So Peirce repeatedly claimed. Whatever happens to accompany the process of thinking but has no specifiable contribution to the fixing of belief does not belong to the nature of thought. The aim of thought in action is, in Peirce's own words, "the attainment of thought at rest." Belief is the end of the line and thinking is the medium through which we attain that end. In view of the fact that thought is a special activity with its own goal, it cannot be identified with consciousness or with merely being aware. Thinking in the relevant sense is not something that is always going on; it is called forth on certain occasions so that it has a reason for coming into play and a goal as well. Thought must be understood through its function — the production of belief.

What is belief? Like many short and seemingly simple questions, this one has an answer which is long and difficult. In Peirce's formula, belief is an awareness which appeases or dispels our doubts and results in the establishment of a habit or rule of action. We are, for the most part, creatures of instinct and habit; we carry out our tasks in accordance with our training, and doubts arise only when we are faced with an alternative which causes us to hesitate or when our activity is impeded by external circumstances. We are, therefore, already acting in accordance with beliefs whenever we act habitually. These beliefs are called into question only when we hesitate in our action or are "not sure" what to do. Hesitancy and doubt in rational beings lead to the attempt to escape from the uneasy situation. Doubt, in short, leads to inquiry or the conscious turning of our mind to the situation and the problem it harbors. If thinking of the focused reflective sort is called forth on the occasion of hesitancy or some doubt about existing belief, its function must consist in the overcoming of hesitancy and doubt or the establishment of a new belief which will be adequate to the new situation. Thinking takes on the role of settling belief because it comes into play whenever old belief is called into question by some hesitancy or failure in action. Thought comes to rest in fixed belief; but every belief must issue in action·so that the deed becomes the final "upshot" of thought. The relation is reciprocal; behind every deed there is ultimately a thought and this is the sense in which action implies belief. Belief, on the other hand, insofar as it must lead to the establishing of a habit, is incomplete without the consequent action and in this sense belief without action is empty and dead. Acting means that we believe something; believing something means that we are required to act.

How does this analysis help us to understand Peirce's theory of meaning, especially his idea· that we must look to those sensible effects which conceivably have "practical bearings"? A clear idea of a thing is an idea which embraces the behavior of the thing; if it is *hard*, it will do certain things under certain circumstances which *soft* things will not do; if it is *soluble* we shall expect it to dissolve, and we shall expect *insoluble* substances to resist solution. Our idea of a thing is not clear unless it contains these patterns of behavior. Even more important, however, is *our own behavior*, including our expectations. A clear idea encompasses not only the behavior of the thing but also the whole range of actions and reactions which we make or prepare to make when confronting that thing. An edible mushroom is one which we expect to eat without ill effects; our idea of that mushroom will include the idea of those motor activities called forth by confrontation with the thing. The idea of the inedible mushroom will embrace different ideas of behavior on our part as well as on the part of the mushroom itself. The meaning of "practical bearings" here is that we must translate the properties we think of when we contemplate the idea of the thing into the behavior of the

thing — the ways it will "work" — *plus* our own behavior
when we are in the presence of the thing or have dealings with
it. Chiefly, "practical" meant for Peirce *practice* or action and
it seemed to him, as it did later to James, that the surest way
to be clear about our meanings is to translate them into action. Peirce went so far as to claim that there can be no difference between two ideas or theories which cannot be translated into difference of actions, either in the object itself or in
our responses to it.

There is no denying that use of the term "practical" in this
connection has been the source of much confusion. Not only
is there ambiguity in the term itself, but that ambiguity was
exploited, sometimes without conscious intention, by pragmatic philosophers. Peirce tried to control the meaning of the
term more rigorously than James did, but by Dewey's time it
became necessary to reassess the whole situation. The ambiguity involved is readily seen. In one sense, "practical"
simply means, as its derivation from the Greek *praxis* implies,
action or behavior which is in some way informed by an idea
or a pattern. In this sense, all human action and regular behavior is "practical," and in so describing it we imply nothing
further about its particular nature. In another sense, "practical" means the immediate relevance of some idea or operation
for the achieving of some end. The practical course of action
is the one which will make a difference in bringing about the
result. Also included in this sense is the idea of *facility;* the
"practical" tool is the one which is best fitted for the function
it has to perform and increases the chances of success. An
action which could legitimately be called practical in the first
sense need not be practical in the second. The second sense
is the one more frequently associated with pragmatism and
with the quality of American life; it is also the sense which
has opened pragmatism to criticism and even ridicule. For

"practical" was often taken to mean the immediately utilitarian or the most convenient in the way of thought or action; it came to be believed, as Dewey saw so well, that being practical meant being crass, materialistic, interested in the short-run expedient without regard to principles of truth and justice. There is another sense of the term which, though less obvious than any mentioned so far, has roots in common sense. When we can detect no difference between two things or two ideas, we say that they are "practically" the same or that "for practical purposes" we need not bother to distinguish between them. Here "practical" has to do with our purpose in view and the degree of precision which it requires. In ordinary circumstances highly precise measurements are not necessary and two pieces of wood which are "practically" the same length may be regarded as equal, since to distinguish them with respect to length would require measuring apparatus more refined than is needed to serve our purpose. On the other hand, should we want to claim that two pieces of wood, for example, do actually differ in length, it becomes necessary to find a *practical* way, an instrument and a specific procedure, of showing the difference. Failure to do this is failure to support our claim. There is no difference between two elements which does not show up as a practical difference, that is, a difference which we can detect either in the behavior of the object or in our own reaction to it.

Peirce appealed to all these senses of practical at one time or another. The first meaning was assumed without question; the meaning of an idea must be found in action, both our action and that of the object. The third meaning played the major role in his theory of inquiry and of empirical science. A sensible effect which has "practical" bearings or, as he often put it, *conceivable* practical bearings, is one which we can detect through specific operations. Whenever we say that two ideas or theories differ in meaning, we must be able to show differences in the behavior of the things involved and differences in our own conduct when we are confronted with them. Confusion creeps in when it is supposed that Peirce was using the term "practical" in the second sense, the most commonly understood sense, and that he intended to bring all thought under the domination of immediate or narrowly utilitarian goals. Peirce was much less interested than either James or Dewey in the practicality of thought understood in this sense. His main concern was for precision in thought and for the truth about the way things actually work. He was less concerned for the instrumental character of thought and for shaping the world with its help. For Peirce, "practical" did not have the same urgent sense of making things over or of getting things done that it had for other pragmatists.

Peirce was very sensitive to the charge often made by critics that the emphasis he placed on action meant the reduction of thought to something other than itself. His spirited reply to this objection not only clarifies his position but throws further light on the role of reason in the conduct of life. Peirce denied ever having reduced thought to action in the sense of identifying it either with the act of thinking itself or with the resulting act which he often described as the "upshot" of thought. An act, he held, is the most singular of *phenomena;* it is the epitome of singularity in fact and excludes generality. No one acts in general; one performs this or that action, but there is no general act. Thought, on the other hand, always has an element of generality in it, and the concept is especially designed to express that feature. It follows that no concept can ever be identical in meaning with an act; the two may be related intimately, but they can never be identical. Thought may *apply* exclusively to action in the sense previously indicated: all ideas are to be translated into forms of behavior or action, but this is different from saying that thought and action are identical. The general character expressed through an *habit* idea is related to action through habit; no idea is identical with any act taken all by itself. An idea, however, may be identified with a habit or disposition to act in a certain way; a disposition is a general tendency not exhausted in any one action, and it is known directly to the one who has it in the form of a *resolution* to act. A resolution to act may be called a belief; belief is related to action without becoming identical with it, since no one act ever exhausts the meaning of the belief.

Life embraces both belief and action. Each implies the other; when we act, we are expressing habits which are essentially beliefs and when we believe, we are committed to following certain courses of action when the appropriate circumstances arise. The subtleties of Peirce's theory of meaning and belief must not be allowed to obscure the bearing of his position upon the conduct of life. Underneath it all he was wrestling with an ancient problem and one which has appeared *** with special force in American life — what is the role of reason in the formation of our beliefs and how do theories intervene in the actual practice of living? All the pragmatists addressed themselves in one way or another to that basic question. It is a difficult question to answer, but in dealing with it we have the consolation at least that it is a vital one, a question of the sort which Dewey classed among the "problems of men," in contrast to those more academic questions which must be regarded exclusively as the "problems of philosophers."

Starting as James did with our actual behavior and conduct, Peirce discovered that belief is a more subtle affair than is often thought. It involves more than contemplating an idea or proposition and it goes beyond *saying* that we believe. Genu-

Calvin

ine belief must be tied to action. There is a touch of Calvinism
in such a view; on the American scene it goes back at least
to Jonathan Edwards and it was the basis of the Puritan concern for sincerity. Since we all have the capacity to deceive,
ourselves as well as others, belief must have some overt and
public signs attached to it; it must be subject to a test. It
cannot exist only in the inner and private recesses of consciousness; we need to have some public way of finding out
whether we really do believe a given idea or doctrine. Peirce
saw the truth in this early tradition and he revived it, as did
pragmatism generally, by tying belief to action. While belief
establishes in us a habit which shapes our actions, doubt —
the contrary state — has no such tendency. Doubt means uneasiness and lack of resolution — it is a state from which we
seek to free ourselves. Doubt has its own power of moving
us, but it is different from the force exercised by belief. Doubt
impels us to *inquiry* and to the discovery of means for overcoming itself. Through inquiry our doubts are dispelled and
belief takes their place. Belief is the ground from which we
act; doubt stimulates us to find that ground through inquiry.

Doubt as well as belief may have a spurious form. Here
Peirce touched a central problem having to do with the relation between science and everyday life. Genuine doubt as it
appears in the living experience of the individual means a
struggle; it means the felt opposition between an established
belief and new ideas, evidence, and new beliefs. Peirce was
critical, even scornful, of general resolutions to doubt of the
sort put forth as a maxim by Descartes. If belief is not the
same as merely saying that we believe, doubt is also not the
same as saying that we doubt. It is not, moreover, the same as
a general resolution to doubt everything in wholesale fashion.
Genuine doubt is based on reasons which call our previous beliefs into question. Since it is based on reasons, doubt can be

overcome only through a critical process which aims at disclosing the error in those reasons or in confirming them by establishing a counter-belief. Doubt, being a state of uneasiness and irresolution, cannot be stable; it stimulates us to find a way of passing out of it. Genuine doubt is deeply embedded in human life and its fate. *The natural science + doubt*

Peirce, however, was aware that the enterprise of natural science was not born of genuine doubt in his sense at all. We did not, that is, wait until there arose in the natural course of events the sort of vital, deeply felt struggle which is characteristic of genuine doubt. Science requires a large dose of *feigned* doubt and hesitancy; it depends, in short, on running ahead of our genuine doubts, on making and tracing out the supposition that some former belief or theory *might* be mistaken and in asking "theoretical" questions for the purpose of trying out the possibilities. In science we engage in doubting for the purpose of testing many things which the individual investigator, under ordinary circumstances and governed by "practical" purposes, does not really doubt at all. Investigation at the level of microscopic phenomena, for example, may mean seriously doubting the uninterrupted operation of the causal principle, although individual investigators are not likely to have genuine doubts about causal connections at the level of everyday experience. Quantum mechanics may demand doubts about universal causality, but it is not likely that individual scientists harbor genuine doubt as to whether they will fall to the bottom of an elevator shaft should they have the misfortune to fall into one through an open door. They may muster doubts about almost anything under the forced draft of the scientific enterprise; this does not mean that they, as individual persons, actually have genuine doubts about these things. Science involves a theoretical standpoint that is not the same as that of ordinary experience.

The chief value of Peirce's insistence that we pay attention to genuine doubt and to the actual conflict of ideas within the individual consciousness lies in its forcing us to consider the role of thought in living experience. In its critical or reflective form, thought comes into play in response to certain demands of life and its success or failure comes to be estimated in terms of human needs. Were habitual action always effective in every way and were the circumstances of life such that they never contradicted our ideas or thwarted our plans, inquiry would very probably never take place. For under such ideal conditions doubt would not exist and there would be no goad to inquiry. But as it happens in actual experience, our ideas are contradicted and our purposes often come to naught; many of our beliefs are false and our plans misguided. If this is so and if our rational faculty is called into play on those occasions when old beliefs and habits let us down, our reason must have practical business in our life. Instead of a power which is exhausted in the contemplation of things, it is a means of transforming them. Thought has a vital function to perform in life; the old common sense opposition between thinking and acting, between theory and practice, can no longer be regarded as true. Our power to think is a living power to correct mistaken beliefs and to frame courses of action which, because they are based on the most reliable knowledge we have, are more likely to succeed in their aims. Life, insofar as it is informed by conscious experience, is a dynamic interplay between belief, doubt, inquiry, and action. When we fail to grasp the truth or are inept in the carrying out of our aims, we find ourselves thrown into a state of confusion; our minds are not at rest and we are unsure about what to do. The whole logical apparatus of man comes into play in order to cope with the situation. This is what Peirce and the pragmatists meant when they said that thought is practical; it is a means of extricating us from our predicaments and, at the same time, of reshaping as much of the environment as is within our power in order to destroy the factors in the universe that work against our well-being and even our very survival. Peirce laid the foundations for the view that was later developed by Dewey under the name of instrumentalism.

Peirce's interpretation of science follows along the lines marked out by his analysis of meaning, belief, doubt, and inquiry. Since he took science very seriously at the same time that he was aware of the limitations of all theoretical thought, a profound understanding of general scientific knowledge is necessary for a full grasp of his philosophy. Peirce, like many other philosophers, tried to interpret science chiefly as a method or way of performing something. Practicing scientists have not always accepted this view and they are inclined to think of it as a logician's prejudice, but there is no denying that the idea played a central role in the pragmatic way of thinking. Science became for the pragmatists chiefly a matter of method because of their doctrine that thought is a process or means for fixing belief. As soon as it was seen that men have attempted to validate their beliefs in a variety of ways, the question of the superiority of one way over another was unavoidable. Since the question was framed in terms of a contrast between different ways of accomplishing a goal, science came to be interpreted as the best *method* for arriving at warranted beliefs. Peirce, it is true, frequently claimed that belief and true belief amount to the same thing since no one believes what he does not think to be true. As far as actual practice in ordinary affairs is concerned, Peirce was right; when we arrive at the belief which we take to be the right one, our doubt is at an end and we do not *in fact* inquire further. If, for example, our electric lights go out suddenly or unexpectedly our first move is to search for the source of the difficulty and as soon as we are convinced that we have found it, our exploration ceases. The satisfaction of the doubt means the end of the quest and our belief in the solution means believing that the solution is true. But, of course, it may happen that the belief which set us at rest was not in fact true; we may have been mistaken. We come here to a much disputed point. The pragmatists, or at any rate Peirce, did not hold that a belief must be true simply because it satisfies us or because its acceptance has brought the process of inquiry to a close. Insofar as he took science to be a standard critical procedure for fixing belief, Peirce wanted to go beyond the habits or behavior of any one individual. His theory of science as a self-correcting way of arriving at beliefs goes beyond individual psychology; it points instead to a community of investigators committed to a method of arriving at critical conclusions. Like Royce, Peirce was also attracted by the community principle; for both it provided a means of taking individual belief into account at the same time that such belief is subjected to a critical standard.

Peirce did much to establish the later widespread belief that all claims to truth and knowledge must have a public character, a character, that is, which makes them generally accessible to people other than the one who makes the claim. The fact that in the past a variety of ways of fixing belief had been tried out, and relied upon, led to the question of their relative merits. Setting out from the assumption that the truth must have a universal reach, Peirce cast suspicion on any way of fixing belief which ultimately rests upon private insight or upon the authority of any individual or group. Universality, he thought, can be achieved only if we can find a way of subjecting our thinking to a standard which itself remains unaffected by that thinking. The solution to the problem is found in the *method* developed by natural science. Individuals and individual circumstances may vary; method introduces the element of universality necessary if we are to avoid individual prejudice and caprice. We do not set opinion or belief directly against another opinion or belief; we subject all belief to the universal method of inquiry and test. Here, as in so many other parts of American life and thought, we find the characteristic trust in the proper way of doing something as the only solution to problems of conflict. It is as if one located faith not in the resolution of the problem but in the path by which it was reached.

If the emphasis falls on method, the next question is what are the distinguishing marks of the best way of approach? For at least three reasons Peirce chose the method of science: it involves a procedure which is public and in principle can be followed by everyone; it has a self-correcting character; and it involves many individuals working together in a co-operative enterprise directed by a common and universal goal. The first characteristic is the one most often appealed to in discussions of science, and Dewey was later to make it the foundation of his philosophy. It means essentially that the one making a claim to truth does not put forth the truth he has discovered in his own name and on his own authority, that is, it is not true because he says it or because of any authority attaching to him as an individual. (Although in actual practice the "expert witness" will often find that others accept his opinion simply because of his standing or achievement in some field of knowledge.) In putting forth a claim to truth, the individual following the method Peirce recommends puts forth simultaneously the way in which he arrived at his result and the data on which it was based. In principle, that is, as long as we can bring with us the necessary knowledge and skill, everyone can follow out the course of the investigation for

himself. The great empiricist principle of "seeing for yourself" is here translated into a public method. Making the entire procedure public means that others can follow along the
same path and see whether it leads to the same place. From a
logical point of view, the fact that not everyone is actually
able (or has the interest or the opportunity) to repeat the
process in question for himself, says nothing against its public
character. We are often guilty, though, of forgetting that
insofar as an individual is unable to repeat the process for
himself, he must "trust" the scientific community. He walks by
faith, not sight.

Peirce was not unaware that other ways of establishing belief, the method of authority either in state or church, and the
method of tenacity as he called it, might claim to have a public procedure in the sense that they could point to the source
of their authority or, as in the case of tenacity, to the reasons
why it is imperative to cling to a belief regardless of the evidence. Peirce's answer is that such methods, if they can be
called methods at all, do not put us under any constraint; they
cannot be wrong because the authority will always establish
its own validity, and we can always cling to a belief if that is
our resolution. There is no possibility of being subject to
correction because there is no possibility of error. But this fact
is precisely the source of a difficulty; it goes against the re-
quirement that we have a standard upon which our thinking
has no effect. The standard in these cases is completely within
our own control.

The second characteristic of science is relevant at this point:
the self-correcting nature of the method. Peirce laid great store
by this feature; when there is any doubt about the validity of
a conclusion reached in science, a process of inquiry must be
started which involves the use of the same critical method.
The self-correcting nature of the procedure is supposed to

reside in the fact that any conclusion reached is still subject to further review at the hands of those committed to following the method. The aim is to replace less adequate with more adequate conclusions and to do so without going beyond the boundaries of the method itself. The superiority of the approach is found in the fact that in addition to allowing for the detection of error, it allows for its correction through further application of the same method.

Peirce understood the method of science in a broad sense. He did not suppose, as many do at present, that science means simply physics or mechanics; science was for him the rigorous following out of empirical method regardless of the subject matter. It means beginning with experience and the problems arising out of doubts which present themselves in the course of our attempt to understand and manage the world in which we live. Inquiry is started with questions and problems and fostered by our creative response to them in the hypotheses we propose for resolving those problems. It is carried further by the techniques of deduction which permit the derivation of consequences that can be checked by appeal to events in the world. The relevance of Peirce's theory of meaning can be seen at once. If the meaning of our hypothesis, according to Peirce's theory of meaning, is to be made clear by developing its practical consequences, then that meaning will take the form of actions and events. The testing of an hypothesis becomes a matter of discovering the extent to which our predictions about the way things *will behave* is confirmed or refuted by the way they *actually do behave* when subjected to experimental tests. In principle this process which begins with a question posed by a doubt, goes on to the proposal of an hypothesis or resolution, which is then translated into future behavior and finally checked with actual behavior, is applicable to any subject matter. The ideas which go to make up hypotheses will, of course, vary in precision depending upon what we are talking about. Hypotheses about the density of things, for example, will be more precise than the hypothesis of God as the co-ordinator of all the types of order which the universe exhibits. But in principle there is to be no division according to subject matter where science is concerned; there are only differences in precision. Hence Peirce could speak as much of empirical inquiry into the nature of prayer and its effects as into the behavior of electrical or magnetic phenomena.

The third characteristic of science — the fact that it involves a community of investigators — played a major role not only in Peirce's theory of science but throughout his entire philosophy. He saw that not only is a single individual severely limited in the scope of his interest and in his ability to try out the consequences of many alternatives, but that the application of a method which demands constant review of conclusions already attained must also require the co-operative efforts of many individuals. It is more than a matter of dividing up the work; the community principle has logical foundations. If the method of science is to provide us with a standard of truth which we cannot manipulate according to our individual interests and if it is designed so as to enable us to arrive at conclusions valid for all, we must have a principle of *inter-subjectivity*. We must have some warrant for the belief that a conclusion reached by X can be checked by Y because Y is able to reproduce the *same* phenomena and the *same* conditions under which they were studied by X. The source of the inter-subjective principle for Peirce, and for pragmatists generally, is the *method* of empirical inquiry which is binding upon *all* members of the scientific community. The unity which stands beneath the efforts of all the investigators is provided by the one universal way of procedure. Research carried on by individuals widely separated in space and time can be the basis of warranted conclusions involving mutual checking and counter-checking on each other because all the relevant activities of the investigators are carried on under the constraint of one empirical method. As individuals they are many, as seekers for truth in accordance with empirical method they are one.

There is, as many have pointed out, something of a paradox in this way of solving the problem. Peirce was aware of it himself. On the one hand when we are asked to show the warrant for our belief that we have avoided subjectivism and that we have escaped individual prejudice and self-indulgence, we point to the community of investigators each of whom exercises a critical function over the efforts and results of all the others. But the community is no more than a name or a fiction unless it is well defined in terms of some unifying principle. How shall we identify the scientific community and who are its members? Obviously not just any set of individuals working together. We need to know on what basis the critical community rests and when we have answered that question we shall find that we have gone beyond the community to a principle or ideal which controls and guides it in the pursuit of its goal. This point is an important one. We do not escape the liability of error which the isolated individual brings with him, merely by multiplying the number of such individuals and setting them all to work. Their efforts must be unified in some determinate way, and the principle of that unity is our only guarantee against subjectivism. But that principle is something more than the fact that they work together or co-operate. This is the mistake of those who appeal to a "social" principle in an uncritical way. That principle avails nothing in the pursuit of truth unless we know how the individuals engaged in a co-operative effort actually qualify for their task.

We need, in short, to know the basis upon which the co-operation takes place, the ideal to which it is dedicated, and the standards governing the activity of those who participate. In Peirce's thought it is the *empirical method* which gives the answer; to qualify for activity within the company of scientific investigators is to acknowledge the validity of this method and be willing to be guided by it in practice.

The community of science both is and is not the guarantor of empirical knowledge. This is the arresting conclusion of Peirce's theory. On the one hand, we have no immediately certain and fully guaranteed access to reality; we are finite and fallible beings subject to error and to the temptation to intrude our own interests and prejudices into our results. And since we are subject to error we need to have some way of checking on our claims. Finite beings stand in need of a norm. We seek this norm in the ideal of critical conclusions arrived at through the co-operative efforts of many individuals aiming at the elimination of what is merely private or parochial in our thoughts. The process of critical investigation with its mutual checks and counter-checks is our only strategy against individual caprice and subjective judgment. But the community of critical investigation must itself stand under the constraint of an ideal which defines its nature and purpose. Insofar as this is the case we cannot say that it is the mere presence of many individuals working together which saves us from error; it is rather the unified co-operative effort of individuals *working under the constraint of an ideal* which is our guarantee. Peirce's conclusion is that outside of the community of knowers we have no access to reality; he belonged in this regard to the idealist tradition, which holds that all of our knowledge is conditioned by our human capabilities and limitations. It is not that we know only our own ideas, but that our knowledge of things is mediated by our ideas.

On the other hand, he resisted the conclusion that our

knowledge is no more than mutual agreement such as might be achieved if we all expressed willingness to define truth in one way or agreed to accept certain conclusions as true regardless of the facts. Peirce's community of knowers is no democracy of opinion based on conventional agreement or majority fiat. Instead he thought of the community itself as *destined* to arrive at settled opinion if its members continued to follow the path of empirical method. This is his version of the famous "long run" idea which played an important role in pragmatic thinking. Truth and reality are the limits to which the opinion of the community must converge. The community is under a constraint beyond itself; it is subject to the dictates of "reality," but no individual or even community of individuals has *immediate* access to that reality. It must be approached through the method of hypothesis and test, and the faithful prosecution of this method will lead to a convergence of opinion in warranted conclusions.

We can now better understand in what way the community both is and is not the guarantor of truth according to this scheme of things. In one sense, the community does define both truth and reality, for we have no access to either except through its co-operative efforts. Finite thinkers have no infallible rule of certainty. We may be condemned to have no more than what the community of knowers can attain and its results may seem poor indeed, but there is no other way and no further alternative; the other ways of fixing belief are even more precarious. On the other hand, the community of knowers does not define truth and reality by fiat; its members are under constraint from beyond their private selves, and the method which guides their activity is at the same time the extra-human standard which keeps them from entering their private opinions and predilections in the book of knowledge.

Stating his conclusions in this way does, of course, some

injustice to Peirce. The systematic undercurrent of his thought
is left out and it might appear that he regarded knowledge,
the community of investigators, and empirical method as just
so many independent features of the world rather than as integrated parts of a theory of reality. While emphasis has often
been laid on Peirce's pragmatism and his work in the theory
of logic and natural science, we must not forget his persistent
attempt to express a vision of the whole. All his basic doctrines
were intended to hang together, and he was not far wrong
when he described himself as an "Hegelian in a strange dress."
The drive to connect the diverse runs throughout his thought;
he strove to establish continuity as the basic law of all that is.
His theory of habit as the general tendency to act is bound
up for example with his claim that the universe contains more
than singular facts; his conception of the community of knowers is demanded by human fallibility and the nature of our
cognitive powers; empirical method is determined by the
doubt-inquiry-belief structure of our intellectual life and by
the evolutionary or dynamic character of the universe. Peirce
was not satisfied with merely describing what he saw; he
wanted to uncover the deeper identities and relations which
help us to understand why things are the way they are.
Though many later thinkers have been content to distinguish
things and to hold them apart in the purity of isolation, Peirce
was bent on achieving just the opposite. He had, for example,
a passion for the philosophy of logic and though he was second to none in ability to contribute to discussions of probability, techniques of deduction, and the foundations of mathematics, he would not allow logic to become a formal exercise
completely cut off from things in the world and from the
other doctrines of philosophy. Peirce believed that inference,
implication, classification, and a whole host of logical concepts and operations must be interpreted in a way which

connects them with our theory of reality. Our way of drawing inferences must be consistent with our theory of mind and our doctrine of classes must reflect the structure of things in the world. Though Peirce added much to formal logic, he would have rejected current notions according to which logic has no essential connection with the ultimate nature of reality; at present it is no more than a calculus based on formal implications. This development surely would have distressed him.

In keeping with his interest in discovering the connections between things, Peirce developed a speculative metaphysic which is remarkable both for its originality and for its insight into ancient truths. We need to remember that in Peirce's time the major theme underlying all discussion of a philosophical nature was *Evolution*. A theory of such revolutionary character was bound to be a focal point for thought, especially when it very early ceased to be merely a biological theory and became an account of the entire universe. For many it became a touchstone for deciding the answer to all questions about nature, man, and God. Every serious philosopher of the time responded to the challenge of evolution; Peirce was no exception. He had his own interpretation of evolution according to which reality develops from less order to more through a process requiring both freedom and chance. He went further than most and attempted to connect evolutionary development with love, with harmony, and with creativity. The most striking aspect of Peirce's theory is its pointed opposition to the struggle and conflict almost universally associated with the evolutionary view of both human and social development. In a manner which once again illustrates the free, spontaneous, and thoroughly unorthodox manner in which essentially Christian ideas were adapted by philosophers, Peirce undertook to use the concept of Love, *agape*, found in the New Testament as the foundation of his theory of cosmic

evolution. Peirce's Agapasticism * — another of his barbarous
expressions — is the result; it marks one of the original and
exciting parts of his metaphysic.

As Dewey was later to emphasize, the theory of evolution
represented an abrupt reversal of many traditional beliefs. It
meant the triumph of change over fixity. And its rapid extension by the Spencers and the Huxleys to a theory of the nature of all things meant unrest and conflict in religious, philosophical, ethical, and social thought. The theory, or rather
the generalized form of it, may even be said to have created
more vigorous discussion outside the natural sciences than it
did in the discipline for which it was first intended. Evolution,
as Jacques Barzun has well pointed out, had magic in the very
idea. The notion of a process which had been taking place
through unimaginably long stretches of time, and in which
the concrete results had been achieved through millions of
infinitesimal changes, fascinated the mind of the nineteenth
century. On the basis of such magic many were prepared to
abandon beliefs which had maintained themselves for centuries. Peirce tried to relate the new to the old and to perform
the function of synthesizer. He was ready to accept the scientific theory, and he was better acquainted with its scientific
foundation and implications than most, but he had numerous
questions of a philosophical sort about the proper interpretation of the process as a whole. He refused to accept uncritically some of the supposed consequences of the theory and, as
a good philosopher should, he avoided confusion between
scientific explanation and philosophical interpretation.

The underlying issues, apart from the more spectacular but
in the end less profound conflicts between biblical literalism
and the Darwinian account of the cosmic process, concerned
the status of man in the universe, the possibility of human

* See note to page 6.

freedom, the place of purpose in the scheme of things, and, not least, social and economic problems arising from the application of the theory of natural selection to the social order. Peirce had something to say about each of these issues. His comprehensive view is expressed in the three principal doctrines of his philosophy (which he designated by ludicrous names derived from Greek words): the doctrine of chance (*Tychism*), which treats the ancient problem of freedom and order on a cosmic scale; the doctrine of continuity (*Synechism*), which deals with the interconnectedness of things; and the doctrine of evolutionary love (*Agapasm*), which interprets the purpose of the cosmic process, especially as it becomes clear through history. The details of these doctrines are too intricate for summary treatment and it cannot be said that they were well enough known in their own time to have exerted any great influence. In some important respects, the theory of evolutionary love sums up the others; it will serve our purposes best to concentrate attention on it alone.

Peirce acknowledged the possibility of three modes of evolution: the Darwinian form or development by fortuitous variation; the necessitarian doctrine or development through mechanical causation; and his own version of evolution through creative love. Although he regarded his own view as the most adequate of the three, Peirce was not unwilling to recognize elements of truth in the other positions. He often described them as degenerate forms of agapasm.

Peirce has his own logical and metaphysical objections to the Darwinian form of evolution, but he seemed to be even more exercised over the social implications of the position. Evolution and the struggle for existence went hand in hand. Progress — and all development in the heyday of Darwinism was regarded as progress — was supposed to result from every individual striving for his own gain and using every opportu-

nity possible for advancing his own interest against those of
others. "Every individual for himself, and the Devil take the
hindmost!" is the way Peirce summed up this outlook. He
called it the "Gospel of Greed," and he was more sensitive
than most philosophers and scientists to the subtle hypocrisy
which sought to mask this gospel behind the old sophistry that
private vice is public benefit. The brutality sanctioned by this
way of portraying human life seemed to him the very opposite
of the spirit of love brought into the world through Christianity. Though Peirce was much interested in reconciling conflicts between religion and science, he rejected any reconciliation between Christianity and what came to be known as
"social Darwinism." The latter seemed to him the same as
unlimited selfish individualism made the more potent because
its advocates clothed their creed with the sacred covering of
science. Peirce sought to combat this tendency.

The theory of evolutionary love is an attempt to make the
Christian virtue the basis of a cosmology and an interpretation
of the course of history. It is a doctrine of God at the same
time. Peirce saw that love cannot be the logical opposite of
hatred, for in that case Satan would become a co-ordinate
power, a conclusion which Christianity always resisted and
one which distinguishes it from every form of dualism. Love
must be capable of embracing its opposite within itself as an
imperfect form of its own perfection. This means that God
loves even the powers that oppose his nature and that he seeks
to transform them through his love. Love has a peculiar movement; it creates independence, or rather makes its creations
have a being of their own, and at the same time limits them
all by demanding that they exist together in a harmony. Love
means sacrifice, which is the opposite of self-seeking; it is the
principle of an evolutionary philosophy because without love
nothing has the environment conducive to growth. On the

other hand, Peirce did not think of love as entirely *sacrifice;* its positive aspect is the fostering of another's growth and perfection.

In Peirce's view evolution belongs primarily to life and mind; the cosmos is capable of further evolution only insofar as it retains the character of mind. This latter thesis, so often found in the forms of modern idealism, had a novel meaning in Peirce's philosophy. Reality has no sharp breaks in itself; polarities and dichotomies illustrated in such pairs as mind and matter, subject and object, universal and individual, Peirce regarded as differing only in degree. Continuity is the true nature of all that exists; old absolute distinctions are replaced by a scale of intermediates with limiting or ideal cases at each end. Peirce could speak of matter as "frozen mind" by which he meant an idea which has become so completely embodied in the habit or tendency to behave in a certain way that it no longer has any freedom or possibility of development. We need to recall the theory of meaning and the connection between the meaning of an idea and the behavior which exhibits that meaning in a public form. The living idea issues in habit or a general tendency to act, retains freedom, and does not become so completely ossified into settled habit that it can no longer grow and develop. Matter, on the other hand, is an idea which has become so habituated that it can do no more than repeat itself or exhibit a mechanical response. Matter must be regarded as a limiting case in view of the fact that Peirce often expressed doubts about the possibility of a purely mechanical response. Like Whitehead, he was not sure that anything is absolutely without life and freedom; his own doctrine of continuity, moreover, prevented him from saying that the limiting case is fully realized. In comparison with life in its more immediate form which grows and is free from purely mechanical behavior, matter is "hidebound" and frozen into the pattern of acting determined by its original idea or form. It tends to do no more than repeat itself, even if never exactly.

The universe, insofar as it has fallen to the level of frozen mind, is beyond the power of evolutionary development. Peirce's belief that order itself evolves as a result of chance (one aspect of the Darwinian thesis which Peirce accepted) means that further development is never possible without an element of chance or "play" in the system. Peirce, like many others then and now, could not see how a thoroughly mechanical view of things is consistent with an evolutionary view. Evolution means development and growth along certain lines; it does not mean mere change. A mechanical view according to which everything must do no more than repeat its former behavior on each new occasion cannot account for the phenomenon of growth. Growth requires freedom, variation, and what Peirce called "chance." To say that reality is capable of evolution at all is to say that it is capable of growth; reality which has become so completely habituated in its behavior as to merit the name of "matter" cannot evolve. Since this case is never perfectly realized, however, all reality may be said to evolve to some degree.

It is necessary to take the foregoing analysis seriously because without it one cannot understand Peirce's claim that evolution takes place only where there is life and mind. We can speak of the evolution of the universe at large because all reality is involved in chance and freedom; dead matter, or an idea which has become so thoroughly habituated that it exactly repeats itself, represents a limiting case. No dead matter actually exists. Peirce repeatedly described his theory of evolutionary love as a law expressing the development of "mind" and if we are to avoid taking this in a narrow and subjective sense we must understand that by "mind" he meant, in addition to the elementary character of feeling, habits or general tendencies which have not fallen to the level of mechanical repetition. Evolutionary love is growth, development, and creativity in the direction of perfecting things and bringing out their potentialities and values; it is the opposite of selfish competition, which identifies progress with an advantage gained by one being through the destruction of other beings.

Peirce set forth the ideas basic to the philosophical outlook which came to be known universally as pragmatism. William James was correct in describing Peirce as the originator of the new way of thinking, although, as we now know, there was much confusion over who had first used the term "pragmatism." But though Peirce was the initiator, his thought was not designed for a wide audience. Much of what he wrote was published in scholarly journals and his difficult terminology was too much for the average reader. His interest was, in the end, scientific and technical. If he was the architect of pragmatism, he was surely not its prophet. And a philosophy with so much bearing on ordinary life and experience could not remain locked up in periodicals; it demanded popular expression. That task fell to William James.

II

William James: PURPOSE, EFFORT, AND

THE WILL TO BELIEVE

William James was remarkable both as a thinker and as a
man. He published books that came to be read all over the
world, and he was untiring in his devotion to friends and colleagues alike. Though he stood in the line of American philosophers for whom the academy is the chief place in life, he
managed to avoid the major failing of academic life — pro-
fessionalism. James, in fact, fought hard against vested intellectual interests and decried the tendency of the academic
mind to follow well-worn paths for fear of appearing incom-
petent, unscholarly, or both. His letters are filled with barbed
witticisms aimed at pedantry and scholastic cant.

James's interest in keeping close to experience and in avoiding views of reality which shape things in order to fulfill the
demands of some philosophical system was not without its
shortcomings. James was surely the most direct, outspoken,
and, we may say, "unqualified" of the pragmatists. This meant
that he often said more than could be defended with responsible arguments. In fact, in his great passion to show the importance of seemingly abstruse ideas for human life and conduct, he frequently overlooked important differences and confused the similar with the identical. Perhaps these are some

of the prices to be paid for an immediately relevant philosophy. Someone has suggested that James wanted to see the results of his ideas as soon as he had expressed them; there is a truth in this suggestion and it accounts at least in part for his tendency to move so quickly from the spoken to the written word. Many of James's papers have an air of simplicity about them which is deceptive, a tone which makes us feel that all previous thinkers complicated matters unnecessarily. This impression arises from his often printing an address just as it had been delivered to a live audience. This practice helps to explain why his writings sometimes contain contradictions and confusions. A careful reader will detect them, whereas they frequently escape the attention of the listener in the lecture hall. There are devices to be used in communicating ideas — especially reflective ones — to a live audience which bewilder a reader when they are transposed to the printed page. There can be no question of the strength of James's passion for making us understand the common bearing of uncommon things, but there was a price to be paid for this virtue and the later pragmatists had to pay it in the form of amending, toning down, and correcting what he had to say.

Reading James is strenuous and not at all as easy as it is supposed to be. The reason is, happily, a creative one. His writing is a continual appeal to the individual to consult his own experience as a means of understanding and testing the ideas being placed before him. A good deal of analysis and observation on the part of the reader is called for; if he does not supply it, many of James's views are likely to appear exaggerated, oversimplified, or simply false. The sense, moreover, of always being in touch with what the ordinary person uncorrupted by philosophical subtlety would say or believe about a given issue gives James's writing an air of confidence, and even of certainty, that can be misleading. In many cases

he was able to bring to the discussion of old issues the fresh-
ness of new experience, or of familiar experience ignored because of the need to maintain professional positions, but in numerous places his confidence was misplaced. He was frequently
naive and uncritical; the most glaring example is his total
failure to see the ambiguity in his crucial doctrine that a distinction or difference in thought must "make a difference" in
experience. Nor did it occur to him that the problem of *judgment* in every region of life is just that of knowing how to decide whether a difference "counts" or not, whether, that is, a
difference is relevant for the purpose at hand. James constantly wrote as though one had only to consult "experience"
as one consults a timetable in order to find the answer. If this
were the case, sound judgment would be less rare than it
obviously is. But no criticism can alter the fact that James
made philosophical ideas available to a wide circle of readers;
even more important, he gave classic expression to a way of
thinking which, more than any other, deserves the title, "American."

Pragmatism stands as America's first indigenous philosophy,
and William James's version of pragmatism is the one with
which the largest number of people both at home and abroad
seem to be acquainted. His position, expressing both a point
of view and a solution to many classical philosophical problems, is no mere reworking of old ideas, but a fresh distilla-
tion of experience acquired on the American scene. Trusting
to his own experience and armed with the characteristically
American concern for the vitality, variety, and challenging adventure of the world, James developed a philosophy of pluralism, radical empiricism, and voluntary assent. If Peirce's view
of things was distinguished by his passion for logic and the
universality we associate with mathematics, James's outlook
was marked by a subordination of logic and the claim that

living experience cannot be contained in any form of universal reason. While Peirce waxed eloquent over the need for a community of knowers and believers, James defended the uniqueness and irreducibility of the individual self. The hallmark of James's pragmatism is its uncompromising belief in each person's right, and even duty, to take his own experience seriously and to use it as a touchstone for thought and action.

James's thought has often been characterized as "voluntarism" — the doctrine that effort, activity, and will have primacy over the acquisition of theoretical knowledge — and this judgment can stand if it is properly qualified. While it would be an error to attempt a reduction of James's philosophy to a neat system or to the proportions of a single idea, it is surely possible to describe the *heart* of his thought as a consistent voluntarism. Human intentions, purposes, plans, and goals are the dominant powers in his universe. Even the God described in his "piecemeal supernaturalism" is distinguished not for any sublime or pure "qualities," but by his relentless activity against the forces of evil and limitation. God struggles constantly, even with limited resources, to make the world a better place in which to live.

Like many of his contemporaries, James was vitally interested in the basic human problem posed by the evolutionary view of the world. What status in the scheme of things is to be assigned to the human mind and its products — ideas and intelligent actions? Is consciousness or mind, man's power to be aware of himself, to think general ideas, to remember and anticipate, to set goals and seek to realize them, a mere spectator or "epiphenomenon" which only accompanies physical processes as a silent witness without having any causal efficacy of its own? * This question and its many implications formed the basis of James's early philosophizing. His answer

* "Are We Automata?" *Mind* IV, 1879; *Princ. of Psych.* I, 140.

embraces not only the voluntarism previously mentioned but also his pragmatism, his theory of truth, and his idea of experience.

If we consider what the evolutionary idea meant within the intellectual climate of James's time, we can see at once why the human mind in both its intellectual and moral aspects should have presented a major problem. Survival in an environment unable to sustain all the living creatures within it calls for the development by the organism of those traits which enable it to overcome the forces that would eliminate it. Surviving characteristics and structures must therefore have functions that contribute in some way to the preservation of life. James, of course, did not accept the view that the *only* function of the human mind is to aid in survival by adjusting or "corresponding" to the outer environment. But he did, for example, in the essay on Herbert Spencer's definition of mind, expose the teleological principle implicit in such a theory. He could agree that consciousness serves a final purpose, but not that its function is merely that of contributing to survival. Consciousness brings its own goals into the picture and thus must consider the quality and direction of life beyond that of bare existence. It adds, in addition, the element of determination and moral resolution — "We *shall* survive!"

The important point, however, is the inevitability of the teleological idea; even if we regard consciousness only from the standpoint of survival, James would say that we are still involved in asking for its contribution to some end or goal. In many early writings, he expressed his conviction that unless the human mind is to be set aside as a "vestigial" organ, it must play some genuine and indispensable role not only in the conduct of human life but also in the course of the world's history. We need, James thought, a view of man's consciousness which will allow for its real efficacy in the world, and a view of the world that is plastic and open enough to allow for the intervention of man's ideas. At the heart of the American experience is the belief that the face of nature can be civilized through the ingenuity and effort of man. A theory of consciousness that has no room for either purpose or effort is unable to meet the need. The source of his dissatisfaction with current mechanist and epiphenomenalist theories of consciousness was their tendency to take the mind as no more than a passive spectator, an unimportant by-product of physical forces. Mind and will — "the experience of activity" — are, on the contrary, powers that are well adapted for active intervention in the temporal process. Their role is not that of watching the world pass by, but that of helping to change it and, if need be, remake its processes and events. In James's favorite phrase, consciousness and will "make a difference"; without *their* influence the course of things would not be what it is. (If we turn from James and consider the entire course of American philosophical thinking over the past three-quarters of a century it is clear that nothing has been more vital than a theory of mind which allows for the transformation of both nature and human society.)

James's philosophy must be recovered by sifting many essays and reviews, as well as books constructed from series of such essays. Like the pluralistic universe he envisaged, his thought does not have the unity of a single system, but it does have a *main drift* that cannot be missed. The nerve of his view is that philosophy, in the shape of a dominant outlook on man and the universe, reaches down into the most immediate concerns and activities of life. Philosophy is neither a luxury for those with leisure nor a learned ornament of scholars; it is for men in every walk of life the ultimate guide of human conduct. The view a man holds on questions of the most basic sort — man's freedom and the existence of God — makes a difference in the course of his individual life and the fate of his historical epoch. Ideas have power; but they do not derive it solely from their logical or intellectual content. To be effective, ideas must become related to human needs and they must enlist the human will. What we believe and the way we act are interdependent; this most essential pragmatist principle is intimately bound up not only with the theory of meaning and the doctrine of truth but also with the indispensability of philosophy itself. The ideas through which we express our ultimate convictions make themselves felt because they are guides of our feelings and our will. This is the essential meaning of the doctrine that ideas are "plans of action."

James's pointed criticisms of "intellectualism" are well known. Though he sometimes used the term in a technical sense to denote a particular theory of knowledge or of mind, more often than not it stood simply as a symbol for those attitudes and views which he stamped as "tender minded." No doubt he often had "Hegelism" in mind too; by this he meant the "block universe," or completed whole of being, as well as an all-encompassing knowledge attained by a mind essentially unencumbered by temporal or historical limitations. Many philosophers had begun by assuming that human reason is a wholly autonomous power uninfluenced by human interest and desire. James began, instead, by seeking to discover the "motives for philosophizing." Philosophical reflection belongs to an individual thinker and it arises within the framework of his individual purposes and plans. Philosophical thinking is not born of intellectual curiosity; it has the task of understanding things so that we have the sense of being at home in a world no longer strange. All thought, but especially that which occupies itself with ethical, religious, and metaphysical issues, is seen as connected with the aims and hopes, the fears and desires, of the one who does the thinking. We do not just think or happen to be interested in knowing; human life tends toward some view of the world because life itself requires meaning and coherence in order to exist. This holds true not only for a view of the external world, but also for a view of the nature and destiny of the thinker himself.

One most important consequence of tracking down the "motives" behind our thought is the sharp restriction that comes to be placed on the idea of a purely theoretical attitude. The older rationalisms defined rationality as a comprehensive system of rational connections and understood man as endowed with a theoretical interest in gaining full knowledge of that system. By contrast James understood rationality through its function in the life of the individual thinker. When James spoke of the "sentiment" of rationality, he did not mean that reason is to be replaced by feeling, but rather that the empirical meaning of a rational world is one in which the self feels "at home" and is able to act in an orderly way. The orderly universe, one in which there are grounds for expecting that certain kinds of events will continue to take place, is viewed by us as rational not because it realizes an eternal rational ideal, but because it provides us with a basis for action and gives us a sense of familiarity. Mystery leaves us in a state of uneasiness; when we have sorted things out and found them to be of certain known kinds, we have the satisfaction of confronting the identifiable, the known. Yet we can never complete the process and especially we find that we are unable to remain content with the explanations. The brute datum of existence over against non-existence still remains and we are forever confronting the fact that we do not find a final reason why we have *this* particular universe and state of affairs rather than nothing at all. James's entire discussion in "The Sentiment of Rationality" is of the first importance for interpreting his thought because it reveals the *speculative*

thrust underneath a surface which appears to be all practicality. The fact is that he saw man as a being unable to avoid
ultimate questions, questions going back to the foundation of
all things. But, like Kant, James did not believe that we can
satisfy our theoretical impulse by means of a rational system.
The rationality of the world cannot therefore be wholly a matter of *philosophical* comprehension. So far we can go and no
farther; from that point we must turn to our moral and aesthetic concerns.

Consistent with this view, James went on to ask what sort
of world would satisfy our practical concerns. Once again the
rational world is seen as the one which fulfills certain demands
of life. When we consider ourselves not primarily as knowers
of things, but as practical agents who make decisions and seek
to shape the course of events, we come to regard as rational
that world which makes action possible and satisfies our will.
"Man," said James, "needs a rule for his will, and will invent
one if one be not given him." The world which genuinely satisfies our practical impulses — a *rational* world in this sense —
is one that gives our active tendencies something to press
against at the same time that it allows to us some measure of
control in determining the future. James felt that a world
which leaves no room for freedom and has no place for human
effort is a world which will never be accepted by the human
will. Such a world will produce no "sentiment of rationality,"
even if it were to be reduced to a single formula which explains
it to the last detail. The world required for an active being is one
which is stable enough to permit calculation, but not so completely fixed and finished beforehand that there is neither need
of nor room for our efforts. The close interweaving between
mind and will is nowhere more evident in James's thought than
at this point. Our world is strange and unfamiliar to us not
merely because we do not know how to describe it or fit its parts

into categories; it is strange and unfamiliar just to the extent to which we do not know how to *behave* in relation to it. The characteristic American question: What is to be done? or What is our next move? becomes relevant at this point. Our world is neither all fixed and finished apart from us nor is it merely the material for knowledge; it forms an arena in which to act and it is filled with dynamic interactions. To feel "at home" in the world means knowing how things are likely to behave and how we are to behave in the face of them. Familiarity is more than storing up the natures or characters of things in our heads; it means the possession of habitual responses in our muscles!

These ideas do not stand alone; they exist against a background which is at once so important and far-reaching in its consequences that we hesitate to refer to it as just one more concept. It is experience itself. Experience is the final court of appeal and the ultimate matrix within which finite life takes place. To paraphrase a venerable saying, experience is that in which we live and move and have our being. Before one can grasp the meaning of the basic ideas which shaped James's outlook, and much of American life in the twentieth century as well, one must explore his distinctive conception of experience. Experience was so important that he came to identify it with reality itself, a fact well known to readers of his essay, "A World of Pure Experience."

To take experience as a court of appeal is no modern invention. Aristotle and other ancient thinkers distinguished between, for example, those physicians who stressed theories and explanations of disease and those who had encountered, seen, handled, *had experience of,* actual cases. The theory of experience — empiricism as a philosophical doctrine — is much younger. It stems from the Enlightenment and has its roots in the British philosophical tradition. Its main feature is the doctrine that experience is of present fact, colors, sounds, tastes, and so forth, which the individual is now perceiving or has perceived. Experience came to mean the passive, but faithful, record of the presented fact. Experience was identified with what came to the self through the senses and it stretched no farther than the limits of sense perception.

Regardless of the extent to which James subscribed to the British empirical tradition, he was resolutely opposed to at least two of its chief doctrines. These oppositions are of the greatest importance for his philosophical outlook, and the ideas he employed to replace the objectionable features of the older view represent what is unique in his own position. According to orthodox doctrine, experience is always the reception of singular fact — this dog; that particular shade of color; the brown bench standing in this corner — and this means that the *connections between things* are no part of experience. The fact that something is to the left of something else as I view it; the fact that some object is similar in appearance to another; the fact that when I witness an event of a certain kind I am led to expect another event with which it is reasonably connected; all these facts were regarded not as belonging to what we *experience,* but rather as stemming from the operations of our mind or reason on the experienced singular fact. Facts were regarded as severely distinct from each other; each fact is what it is and not another fact. The result is that the connections between things are no part of experience. They are either illusory or pure products of the mind.

James rejected this view. For him the connections and relations between the items of experience belong as much to experience as any of the terms or things do. Experience is not a matter of a passive spectator on one side viewing clear-cut and neatly packaged data of sense on the other; experience is rather a living stream in which the destiny of the self is wrought out. Experience starts, in James's famous phrase, as

"a booming, buzzing confusion," a welter of items encountered, feelings, tendencies, reactions, anticipations, and so
forth; only in the course of time do we manage to sort out
what we encounter, reduce it to some order, and then try to
discover what the world as a whole means and what our life
within it is all about. The connections between things are as
much present in experience as the things themselves; this is
the great lesson of James's empiricism. A celebrated issue will
help to explain the point.

David Hume, speaking for most modern empiricists, ex-
amined what is known as the causal relationship — one bil-
liard ball, for example, striking another and causing it to fall
into one of the pockets — and declared that though we did
"experience" the motion of the one ball, the impact of one on
the other, and the consequent motion of the second ball, we
could not be said to "experience" the *causal connection* or
relationship. Like most hard-headed people, Hume wanted to
"see" causality. The causal connection, he concluded, does not
belong to experience, but must be introduced, if at all, by
an operation of the mind. James rejected this exclusion from
experience of the "connective tissue" between things and argued that closer attention to our actual experience will reveal the presence of relations and transitions. Actual experience is not just a series of disconnected things. He proposed
to examine what he called the "activity situation" as we all live
through it in our own lives.

A man sees a photograph of a house similar to his own but
differing in that it has a back terrace, which his own house
lacks. He conceives the plan of building a similar terrace on
his own premises. His plan will include not only the desired
result but an inventory of the needed materials and a schema
of the actual work to be performed, plus the order in which
things are to be done. As soon as he begins the process of

building he becomes aware of himself as an agent or maker, and as he brings the project to completion he experiences a continuous activity that has produced or brought about the state of affairs that he planned in the beginning. He has experienced causal efficacy; he is directly aware in his own experience of having gone from a plan to its fulfillment in a well-ordered series of steps. James's conclusion is that experience, properly understood, includes not only events and things, but the connections between events and things. Experience does not concern itself with static or fixed objects, each of which exists all by itself without any intelligible connection with anything else.

In refusing to accept as final one particular account of what we actually experience, he was making a plea for a continual return to experience as immediately lived through in order to check the accuracy of any theory. James used a more extensive experience to check Hume's account. He hoped to capture *all* that is encountered or lived through by human beings in the course of life; he was not satisfied with a few selected features such as might serve some special purpose. James, moreover, was suspicious of experience which is so highly "filtered" by preconceptions that many important items are excluded. His so-called "radical empiricism" is the most thorough and rugged empiricism on record. It is a persistent attempt to return to the source and to recover what we actually live through. His interpretation of religion furnishes us with an excellent illustration. Instead of beginning with the traditional empiricist claim that God cannot be found in experience, he set out to find the elemental human experiences which first suggested to men the idea of an infinite and ultimate Being.

Closely associated with his demand that we take all of experience, the connective tissue as well as the terms, was James's insistence that we stop viewing experience as a passive affair.

We come here to the heart of the pragmatists' criticism of the older empiricism. Not until Dewey did we see its full implications, but James made the initial move. The appeal to experience in the philosophers of Enlightenment was an appeal to what is actually sensed as a means of testing the correctness of abstract ideas and principles of explanation. In order to use experience for this purpose it became necessary to interpret it as a *passive* affair, as an affair in which the knowing self keeps itself, its ideas, predilections, interests, out of the picture in order to be a passive recipient of the data presented. Various images were used to express this passivity of the subject; the blank slate of the mind upon which "experience" traces itself or the wax tablet which receives, without adding anything of its own, the impression made by the seal. As over against all this, James held that the experiencing subject is always a creature of interests, plans, and purposes; there is actually no passive subject. Even the aim of being purely passive, assuming that this is the correct approach to the attainment of scientific or purely theoretical knowledge, is itself the expression of a purpose and an interest; it is not the "natural" state of the self.

The philosophy of Francis Bacon, the thinker often described as the father of modern science, furnishes an excellent example of the position to which James objected. According to Bacon the one who experiences is a spectator of things which are "given" to him ready-made. This means that the world of experience is always a world already finished. Although the given things are present to the self and the self to them, by the time the spectator records the event or thing, it is already completed, already in the past. On the Baconian view, experience is of finished products, never of processes. From this vantage point it was an easy step to a "copy" theory of knowing, in which knowledge is the result of passively reflecting or "copying" in the mind what has been met with "out there." The best copy and therefore the most reliable knowledge is the one which has been least distorted by the interests of the self or by the theories of the spectator.

James, upon examining his own experience while bidding each of us to do the same, found at least two errors in this account. While he did not deny all truth to the copying idea, he did hold that we have no more than a limited power to copy what is presented to us. When we see a clock on the wall we can copy (in the sense of have an image of) its round face, its hands, its numbers, but we find ourselves unable to produce the same sort of copy for the power plant of the clock. We cannot copy the energy in the spring which keeps the mechanism in operation. Thus our limited power of copying all that is presented to us suggests that experience is not entirely composed of finished sensible fact, but that it contains as well powers and transitions, tendencies and potentialities, which the senses as such do not disclose. Put in this way, the issue at once becomes clear: Are we to confine experience to the senses and exclude from its domain many important features of the world, or shall we seek an account of experience which is more in accord with what we actually find, even if it means giving up the neat and clear-cut Enlightenment theory? James decided for the latter alternative.

Even more important, James exposed one of the powerful but questionable assumptions of the older empiricism when he saw that its theory of the passive spectator meant that the self must become a theoretical knower and nothing else. On that view the only business of the self in the world is to be engaged in obtaining a purely theoretical view of things. James did not deny that, *under specially controlled circumstances,* such a theoretical knower is both possible and necessary, but he refused to allow that the experiencing subject, as a concrete human being, can be defined exclusively in terms of those special circumstances. The one who experiences is not a disembodied bearer of pure reason, nor a being who goes about with no other purpose than that of copying the world around him. The subject of experience is a concrete person with purposes, plans, aims, and desires and indeed all of the other characteristics familiar to all of us. The desire to possess theoretical knowledge is but one desire among many and, even when such knowledge is attained, the individual person must discover the particular bearing which it may have upon his own conduct and destiny.

James wanted most to emphasize that, in the situation of actual experience, the self is very far indeed from being a passive creature. Each person is endowed with a drive toward self-understanding and self-mastery. Before we can begin to understand anything about the world or ourselves, we must seek to distinguish and discriminate between things; we do not passively register what is there, as so many photographic devices might do. We seek to emerge from that booming, buzzing confusion which is the world, *before* we have gained any understanding of it or any control over it. In order to emerge from a state of virtual helplessness, where we are at the mercy of the world and its whirl of things, we seek to manage the contents of experience by means of names, categories, and principles. These furnish clues to what we are to expect and to the reasons why things are as they are. We who experience must intervene; we must, in short, attack our experience with some definite purpose in view and with some means for accomplishing it. The most elemental of all purposes is that of self-control and self-realization. We seek to be at home in the world, to be delivered from total chaos and contingency; the first steps in this direction are taken when we begin to master our own experience. The gaining of precise theoretical

knowledge of things develops in the course of time. There is
no tendency on James's part to belittle science, but he refused
to allow that a theoretical orientation to things is basic to our
outlook. Prior to that special interest is the more fundamental need of being at home in the world and of becoming clear
about our purpose and place in the scheme of things. These
basic needs of the person are the most important factors in
defining the nature of experience; the conditions for theoretical
knowledge, though important, are not the basic ones. Experience, therefore, is not the same as theoretical knowledge; it
contains the materials for such knowledge, but it is broader
than any selection of its contents.

The placing of the concrete person at the basis of experience
had important consequences for James's thought. Instead of
the passive spectator, we now have a self endowed with purposes and plans. Those purposes and plans are behind every
distinction we draw, every selection we make, and every response we exhibit in coming to terms with ourselves and the
world about us. Purposes may be broad or narrow, trivial or
momentous, but they are always there. When we dip into our
stock of experience, whether past or present, we are guided by
what we are trying to accomplish. Take the case of classifying things. One of the first ways in which we respond to our
experience is by seeking to discover what we are, as we say,
"up against." We want to know what is what and that usually
means knowing the names, the kinds, and the expected behavior of things. Classification plays a large part in the process.
But a view of experience which places theoretical knowledge
and the achievement of science in the foreground will invariably take classification as a primitive intellectual drive, the
drive for knowledge all by itself. It will not see that classification is one of the basic means whereby we become masters of
ourselves and our world. From the standpoint of the concrete

individual, classifying things is a way of becoming familiar with them and thus of reducing the frightening and potentially dangerous world to an order in which he feels more at home. James never supposed that this purpose was merely secondary, no more than a by-product of a more basic theoretical drive. On the contrary, he placed the human concern for being at home in the world in the forefront and used it as the basis for understanding what experience really is. The theoretical concern which can succeed only by ignoring the special interests of the individual self represents a later development in experience. Through it we obtain a precise, universalized picture of things, but that picture is purchased at the price of leaving out many features of what we encounter in experience. James had no interest in undermining the importance of theoretical knowledge, but he wanted it clearly understood that seeking for such knowledge represents *one purpose among others* and that the successful fulfillment of that purpose means the selecting from a richer experience of things just those aspects capable of the most precise formulation. He resisted the tendency of the modern world to identify the whole of experience with the abstracted results of science; science emerges as a result of reflection upon experience, but it is not the starting point of experience nor do its results express the content of experience in a fashion wholly superior to all others.

We must now seek to understand James's three basic ideas — purpose, effort, and the will to believe — within the framework of his theory of experience. Each represents one facet of his brand of pragmatism and each helps to define his philosophy of the individual self in a world that has an "open end." Our plans and purposes provide us with principles of selection within experience, guiding our reason and directing our energy, giving us clues to what is relevant in a given case as well as what is not germane to our interests. If our experi-

ence discloses an unfinished world, a world with a future, with
parts and aspects still in the making, then we shall wonder
whether we may not have a part in the shaping process itself.
In short, we shall ask whether the function of our minds and
of the energy we feel stored within us will not be to influence
the course of things. Just as God is engaged in struggling to
bring about the best states of affairs, so may human beings
exercise effort to realize their own finite goals. The sense of
effort is the sign which tells us that we are creatures of freedom, that our wills are capable of bringing about changes in
the stream of events; we are not passive mirrors of the passing
scene, but agents able to contribute something to the completion of a universe as yet unfinished. Effort, however, would
be of little avail, especially in rational beings, if it were no more
than a blind thrashing about or a haphazard discharge of vital
powers. Our efforts must be guided by our purposes and our
purposes must be framed in the light of our knowledge of
things. Here we see an interplay which stands at the center
of James's philosophical vision; the intimate connection between knowing and believing on the one hand, and effort and
the discharge of energy on the other. Ideas and beliefs held
are worthless and powerless if they lose all connection with
our will; a belief which has nothing to do with conduct is, if
conceivable at all in James's terms, surely lifeless and inert.
Our conduct, on the other hand, cannot be regarded as fully
human unless it is informed by ideas believed in with sufficient
passion and sincerity to make them into well-springs of action.
James sought to express the intimate connection between
what he called "our passional nature" and the beliefs we hold
through his well-known and oft-misinterpreted *will to believe*.
We can penetrate more deeply into James's pragmatism, and
understand his voluntarism as well, if we attend more closely
to his notions of purpose, effort, and the will to believe; these

ideas understood against the background of experience express the essence of his thought.

At the heart of James's criticism of rationalism, the doctrine, that is, of man as a purely theoretical intellect engaged in knowing an already completed world of finished fact for its own sake, was his claim that rationality in human beings is exactly what it is *known as* in direct experience; it is not of such a nature as might be imagined were we constituted differently or were the universe other than it is. Rationality means both a set of powers possessed by human beings and also certain demands which these same beings place upon themselves and upon their world. James, like Royce, expressed doubt about the existence of a "pure intellect." He did not deny that it is possible to have as a purpose the gaining of purely theoretical or disinterested knowledge of things. But he wanted it clearly understood that such purpose represents a special interest, one interest besides others; it is not the expression of the "natural" bent of the human person. For James the exercise of reason, as indeed of every other human faculty, takes place within a concrete and human context. Not only is reason always somebody's reason, but it is exercised on specific occasions under appropriate circumstances. Life and experience are wider than reason, and this means that the purposes at life's base direct and determine all that we think and do. Even theoretical reason does not operate aimlessly; its exercise is controlled by a well-defined purpose, one which is universal and impersonal requiring the individual under its constraint to ignore his own special interests and concerns. The fact that attaining a theoretical view of things requires great discipline and effort, however, suggests that the "natural" drift of thought is not to be defined in this way. Each individual finds himself primarily engaged in working out his own destiny, in hoping to gain a view of himself and the world which gives point to his life. This is his dominant or commanding purpose and, in the absence of specially constructed purposes, all of his energies will be guided by this dominant one.

A disinterested view of things, such as the one that defines natural science, is one of the achievements of man. James not only accepted this, but he made his own important contributions to our scientific understanding of the world. Nevertheless his empiricism and his humanism, his passion to reflect on what actually happens and not what we think should or could happen, and his concern for the fulfillment of the individual self, led him to ask for the *relevance* of our theoretical knowledge, especially in situations calling for choice and action. Here we touch upon a momentous consideration. James was impressed by the boundless character of all pure knowing. If our purpose is really to know the nature of something, there is, in principle, no limit to the number of facts we may proceed to lay bare. Left to itself and guided by no other purpose than that of just knowing, the theoretical intellect is bound to extend itself to an infinity of detail. But the individual self, though he may for a limited time make it his aim to gain such knowledge, still retains his own concerns as a concrete being seeking to work out his destiny. The concern for completed theoretical knowledge does not define his own being as an individual person nor does it exhaust his own purpose. Moreover, many of the situations in which the person finds himself do not allow him the luxury of continuing to discover pure truth without limit or responsibility for its use. The facts of decision and action are facts which make all the difference. That we are unfinished beings living in a world as yet unfinished means that we have practical work to do in the shaping of our world and the transforming of ourselves. Action requires decision and decision means judgment — the selecting of what is relevant and the rejection of what does not count. Decision means a course of action embraced and others set aside. We need, in short, a principle of *selection*. We need to know what is relevant in the specific situation now confronting us. For, as Dewey was later to make plain, a situation gets to be specific by virtue of the fact that it does not involve us in a whole universe of detail at once. Much of what we believe and know at a given time will not be relevant to accomplishing the task at hand. Our problem in concrete experience will be to discover what factors we must take into account and what factors may be safely ignored. The purely theoretical intellect all by itself cannot answer these questions. There is theoretically no limit to the detail it can disclose or to the degree of precision it can attain. "The human mind," said James, "is essentially partial. It can be efficient at all only by *picking out* what to attend to, and ignoring everything else, — by narrowing its point of view . . . Man always wants his curiosity gratified for a particular purpose." * Without a purpose to guide us we should be lost in an infinity. We can, for example, conduct our business in a grocery store without the need of very precise terminology and without going beyond the resources of our ordinary language. In a court of law or in a laboratory, however, we soon discover that precision of language and thought is required which goes far beyond the demands of everyday life. It is the purpose which guides and determines us in every concrete situation. All human talents and capabilities, including our reason, must be exercised in accordance with aims and goals. James's chief objection to the idea of a pure intellect searching for an absolute truth is that such an intellect contains no purpose beyond that of knowing everything and may overwhelm us with an infinitude of detail without providing us with an idea of what we are to select as relevant in a specific situation.

* *The Will To Believe and Other Essays*, p. 119.

In understanding the role played by purpose in James's philosophical outlook, we must be careful to take note of the fact that purposes differ not only in their directions but also in their scope. When James referred to our ideas as "plans of action," he sometimes had in mind no more than a set of specific directions for achieving some definite and quite ordinary result. Our conception of some fascinating and far away place can become a plan of action when we translate it into a set of directions for reaching it and bringing it within our direct experience. But James had a somewhat broader idea in mind when he talked about the purpose of the individual self. Each one of us is trying to understand ourselves and our world, each one of us has certain dominant purposes which guide and direct the whole of life. In redefining rationality as it is experienced in concrete life, James described the person as a being seeking for a view of things which provides us with a familiar world — one in which we feel "at home" — and a world sufficiently predictable to enable us to project future actions with a reasonable guarantee of success. A world so understood gives to the individual self a sense of stability, a "sentiment of rationality." Since, however, we are active as well as thoughtful beings, we seek for a world which has room in it for our own will and effort. We seek a plastic world, one which is sufficiently open toward the future to allow us to shape its course and have a hand in determining what is to come. As concrete human persons, we seek for a "rational" world in both of these senses, a world which is intelligible enough to make us feel at home and a world pliable enough to be responsive to our efforts.

The search for such rationality represents an over-all purpose for human beings; it expresses what James had in mind when he spoke about "life" as an ultimate value. In his well-known statement that whenever logic is in conflict with life, it is so much the worse for logic, he meant to point up the search for an overarching purpose in life as the chief and proper business of the individual person. Whatever else he may do, whatever he may think, believe, or propose as true, must finally be related to his dominant purpose. There are times when James, in referring to the success or failure of a plan of action, meant no more than success or failure with respect to some particular aim or project. At other times he meant the success or failure of the self as a whole in the quest for self-understanding and a purposeful life. In the latter case success or failure has to do with life itself, with the total destiny of the individual.

Failure to distinguish between piecemeal purposes and the purpose of life as a whole has occasioned much misunderstanding of James's position. The distinction was not always kept clearly in mind by James himself. At many points in his writings, from his early paper on "Philosophical Conceptions and Practical Results" to his later religious thought and radical empiricism, James consistently upheld the view that there can be no distinction in thought which does not "make a difference" in experience for someone, somewhere and somewhen. He seems not to have noticed the basic ambiguity in this celebrated doctrine. On the one hand it represents no more than a novel way of stating an old idea, but on the other it expresses a new idea, one which is understandable only if we pay attention to the dominant purpose of the individual. As the expression of an old idea, the doctrine means no more than an appeal to experience. If, for example, I claim that there is a genuine difference between the doctrine that man is free and the doctrine that all events are necessitated by causal laws, I must be able to show that there are specifiable differences in what we shall see, feel, encounter — experience in the broadest sense — if one or the other position is true. James's point is that to distinguish between the two positions in thought without being able to point to the specific ways in which the related experience would differ is to make an idle distinction, a difference which makes no difference. Quite apart from the ultimate truth of this view, it is clear at least in outline: for a distinction between ideas to "make a difference" we must be able to say what difference it does make in what people will experience or, as James sometimes put it, in what conduct people will display. But there is another sense of "make a difference" which can be understood only if we attend to the purpose of individual life as a whole. It is the sense which is expressed in the ordinary question: What difference does that make to me? Here the concern is not with this or that arrangement of the facts, with differences in what people perceive, but rather with "making a difference" in the sense of "has a bearing upon" my dominant purpose in life. There are differences in the world which "make no difference" to me in the sense that I am indifferent to them because I do not see that they are relevant to the achieving of my purpose in life. This is not to say that I am always correct in supposing that these differences are *in fact* indifferent to me; I may be mistaken, and tragically so, in the belief that a given difference in thought passes me by or leaves me where I was before. But the question of being correct in my judgment, or not, is not the main issue. The issue turns on a basic difference in meaning between the two senses of "make a difference." In one case I am concerned with what people perceive and with the way facts are arranged in the world — as in the case of James's well-known illustration about the man going around the squirrel. But in the other case, the *relevance* of a difference in thought or belief for my particular purpose and destiny in life is involved. The first case, regardless of James's emphasis upon the will and conduct, can still be interpreted as a theoretical affair without any necessary reference to the purpose and destiny of the self. But the second case is different; it focuses on the *bearing* of a given idea, thought, belief upon the total course of my life. Making a difference in this case involves my judging whether a difference in thought can or cannot be safely ignored by me; it involves selection and judgment. The first sense of making a difference makes no essential reference whatever to relevance or to the bearing of a difference upon individual purpose. With the second sense it is quite otherwise; there we find the characteristically American concern for the bearing of an idea on the course of someone's life. The tendency in American life to be suspicious of "theories" and of those called "intellectuals" is explicable in these terms. The tendency means uneasiness in the face of ideas, distinctions, and shades of meaning that seem to have little or nothing to do with the course of anyone's life. The demand that every thought have a *cutting edge*, that it have a bearing or make a difference to the purpose of somebody's life, is deeply rooted in the American consciousness. Suspicion and even hostility results when that bearing is not clear. James was, like Janus, reflecting that tendency as it came to him from the past and also giving to it powerful expression for the future.

If James showed great concern for purposes and plans in human life, he was no less interested in their execution. Very early in his career James occupied himself with the problem of determining the place of human will in a world that was becoming more and more interpreted in mechanical terms. In an early criticism of Herbert Spencer, James objected to the "adaptation" thesis and to the doctrine that the human species succeeds only insofar as it can be molded by forces beyond itself to fit an environment that determines it at every point. To counteract such a view, he vigorously maintained that the activity and effort of man are no mere phenomenal appearances in a materialistic universe, but that they make a genuine difference in the course of things. Two fundamental considerations are behind James's contention. First, it is not true that man is a purely passive being capable of no more than an adaptive response. On the contrary, it is characteristic of rational and sensitive beings to anticipate the future and to evaluate the worth of various alternatives when called upon to act. Man is capable of putting forth effort in order to carry out his plans; he is not condemned to wait for everything to happen. Secondly, his effort is not futile because it takes place within an open, plastic, unfinished, and pluralistic universe. James's attack upon the doctrine that the universe is already "all there" as a fixed and finished product has momentous bearing upon his entire philosophy. It is just because the universe is not finished but is still in the making that we are able to find room for the exertion of our own will.

No one was more sanguine than James in believing that individual energy influences the course of history. In a widely read essay, "Great Men and Their Environment" he added his voice to the debate then raging about the proper explanation of the hero and the genius against the background of evolutionary theory. James saw at once that a theory like that of Herbert Spencer, which explains away the individual as a mere product of impersonal forces, could claim no support from Darwin. Spencer's view requires a universal fatalism and it assumes a closed, mechanical universe, whereas Darwin made central to his own theory the concept of *accidental* or fortuitous variation. Following Darwin, James distinguished sharply between factors leading to "spontaneous variation" and those factors which influence the development of such variation after the fact, either sustaining or thwarting its growth. These two sets of factors, he held, are by no means identical, and the selective factors which play their role after the variation has appeared do not suffice to explain the initial variation. For James the extraordinary individual represents just such a spontaneous variation; the environmental factors so much used by Spencer and others in explanation of the individual are operative only after the fact. They have a selective function in relation to the individual; they do not explain his appearance in the first place.

James objected to taking the environment as the necessary and sufficient cause of every idea, feeling, tendency, and predilection of the individual, because such a view takes it for granted that the same factors which determine the future of any of these facts, *once they exist*, would have sufficed to produce them. James was able to point out that on the Darwinian theory the social environment comes into play with its selective function only after a spontaneous variation is on the ground. He urged the same point with regard to mental development. Like Peirce, James saw that before progress can be made in understanding the world and the causes of things, explanations and hypotheses must be proposed. No collection of facts announces the law which connects them. For that individual intelligence is required. Once proposed, an hypothesis can be tested in and through the efforts of a community of investigators; the fate of the hypothesis will be influenced by factors in the social environment. But the terms in which the hypothesis will be tested after the fact are not such as would have been sufficient to produce it in the first place. Unless there is an individual mind to which the solving idea or explanation first occurs, the process of testing and selection will never take place.

It is not only in matters intellectual that James maintained his thesis. The universe is such that throughout the whole range of human activities individual effort makes a difference. Were the world all finished and given once for all, human energy would make no essential difference to the course of events. The feeling of effort would be but a subjective appearance. But neither the world nor man is finished; each has a future into which to move and develop. The emphasis upon the future so characteristic of American pragmatism always points up the importance of a *time for making* or accomplishing something; we do not wait for the future, but anticipate it and seek to determine it. Man is essentially an active being; he is in the making along with his world. He can, moreover, have a hand in shaping the future, since his energy is one of the factors in the process.

In his early psychological studies, James was busy examining the then popular theory that man is but an automaton whose consciousness passively reflects the passage of things without in any way affecting it. He never accepted this theory, but it was not until many years later that his position became clear. In a study entitled, "The Feeling of Effort" (1880), James took the view that the feeling of muscular effort is an *afferent* sensation of a motor response which has *already taken place*. This was the dominant empiricist view and James was willing to go along with it as far as overt behavior is concerned. He did, however, hold out for the "feeling of mental spontaneity" as something which is not afferent and which is a non-sensational real factor in human life. Even if we suppose, he argued, that all the contents of the mind come to it from the outside world, we still have the experience of choosing among these contents, of emphasizing one while setting another aside, of accepting one while disapproving of another. The feeling of activity may be confined to this mental activity, but it is nonetheless real and it makes a difference in what happens in the world. Critics, however, did not agree. If the feeling of muscular effort is no more than the *record* of what has already taken place, why may not the sense of psychic effort be the same? In that case it would be inefficacious, would make no difference, and we should then be left with the feeling of effort without the fact. James took these objections very seriously and continued to consider the question. In 1904 he arrived at his final answer in an address before the American Psychological Association, "The Experience of Activity." His solution calls upon all the resources of both pragmatism and radical empiricism and it involves some reinterpreting of the original question concerning the efficacy of the mind and will in bringing about change.

A philosophy of pure experience must find the meaning of all of its terms in experience open to everyone. It soon becomes clear that in invoking this principle James means to abjure all attempts to find causality beneath or beyond experience as it is actually lived through. He accuses those who take our direct experience of striving and achieving to be no more than a surface illusion, of being guilty of animism, and of invoking "principles" which cannot be justified. His view, on the contrary, credits the experience of activity as an ultimate fact. His own words are eloquent in defense of the thesis:

> Sustaining, persevering, striving, paying with effort as we go, hanging on, and finally achieving our intention — this *is* action, this *is* effectuation in the only shape in which, by a pure-experience philosophy, the whereabouts of it anywhere can be discussed. . . . here is causality at work.*

Genuine efficacy, then, is embedded in experience, in the most ordinary as well as the most sublime. Our sense of effort is no mere record of what happens to us nor the dim reflection of results wrought by unknown powers operating upon us. Real causality is just "what we feel it to be," and the fact that we consciously attend to or are aware of the expenditure of effort only in those situations where the obstacles are severe

* "The Experience of Activity" in *Essays in Radical Empiricism*, pp. 183–4.

68 *William James*

does not argue against the reality of that effort nor the reality of
the difference it makes in determining the course of events.

On a more practical plane — the plane to which James always returns — the doctrine of effort had its fullest significance
for American life through the support it gave to the development of a technological civilization. Like Kant, James moved
back and forth between the extremes of *arguing* for man's freedom or power to introduce novelty into the world and *exhibit-
ing* that power through a spirited call to perform the deed and
carry out the intention. The actual performance is the more
important; whether James succeeded or not in defending the
reality of efficacy and effort in theoretical terms, there is no
doubt that he firmly believed in that efficacy and his writings
induced many others to follow after him. His vision, in short,
gives expression to the typically American interest in transforming the face of nature through knowledge, ingenuity, and
invention. James is Emerson come down to earth. When Emerson declared that if we do not like the world about us, we
should create a new one, he was reminding us that rational
beings need not remain satisfied with the world into which they
are born. But in Emerson's view that new world was to exist
only in imagination or in the inner recesses of aesthetic feeling.
For James the new creation shall have an outer, an "earthy"
form; it will be the product of effort directed toward the civilizing of the face of nature. Since the world is not finished and
is a place where our efforts can be made to count for something, nature can be redeemed from its brute existence. Nature
can be made into a new and more stable habitation through
human ingenuity, by which we can harness its powers and
work through and with them in the shaping of the future.

Since James was interested primarily in the individual person and in the many problems he must face in a changing
world, he did not give his pragmatism the social and economic

orientation which was later to define the thought of Dewey. In this regard James was not the philosopher of America, the great industrial giant. But he pointed the way. That nature is plastic enough to give room to our needs, our desires, and our efforts and that we have sufficient energy to effect our plans and purposes are doctrines which laid the foundations for a more thoroughgoing attack upon nature. They represent the incipient rationale of a technical civilization.

There is no idea in James, or in any other American philosopher for that matter, which is more widely known and more universally misinterpreted than the will to believe. For many, professional philosophers no less than laymen, it has been taken to mean that you not only can, but that you should, believe anything you care to believe and that, with regard to anything you desire to be true, you can force yourself to believe it to be true against all evidence if only your will is strong enough. Perhaps the expression "will to believe" was unfortunate; we know that James later wished he had called his idea by the name "right to believe." In some ways this title would have been more accurate because it points to James's idea that we are *justified* on rational grounds (and in this sense have a "right") in taking certain propositions for true and in acting upon them in advance of rational proof. The term "will" on the other hand, often connotes arbitrariness; it implies belief by fiat or by sheer power unconnected with reasons or grounds. But regardless of the ideas either suggested by or implied in a name, the fundamental notion expressed by the will to believe is most important for James's pragmatism. It would be difficult, moreover, for an impartial observer to deny elements of truth in the idea, even though it obviously has limitations and is open to misuse.

As a preliminary to understanding, several facts must be kept in mind. First, and most important, is James's refusal to leave out of account in the settling of any issue the facts of actual conduct. He would not, that is, allow considerations as to what we might do or ought to do to take precedence over the established facts. In the present case this means that he was more interested in the way in which people actually arrive at their opinions or beliefs, than in the way in which someone may claim that they ought to. Secondly, it is essential that we not lose sight of the intimate connection between belief and action which exists on the grounds of James's pragmatism. Believing is not the same as *saying* that one believes; believing means willingness to act, especially under conditions of risk, in ways dictated by the meaning of the belief in question. Finally, the greatest obstacle to grasping the will to believe is failure to notice the clear limitations placed by James on what he regarded as our right to believe certain propositions if we are willing to take the risks and endure the consequences. The fact is that it is only under certain well-defined conditions that the will to believe becomes operative at all. It is not a blanket policy covering all occasions and it is not an unlimited license entitling us to determine truth as we will.

James assigned the term "hypothesis" to anything proposed to us for belief and then proceeded to distinguish live from dead hypotheses, depending upon whether the proposal appeals to the individual as a real possibility or not. By possibility here, James means willingness to act upon or take the proposal seriously. There may be, for example, no possibility whatever of an individual becoming a follower of the Buddha in which case the proposal to believe in the Buddha is a dead hypothesis from the start. Being live or dead belongs to the hypothesis not in itself, but only in relation to the individual to whom it is addressed. The next question is whether what James called an *option* — the decision between two hypotheses — has a certain character or not. A genuine option is one in which (1) both alternatives involved are live and make some appeal to us, (2) there is no way of escaping the choice, and (3) the opportunity involved is unique and the decision is irreversible. James called an option fulfilling all three conditions one that is *live*, *forced*, and *momentous*. It should be clear already that the will to believe is mightily hedged in by conditions and is very far indeed from being a license for self-indulgence.

The next question is this: To what extent are our opinions rigorously determined by intellect alone, quite apart from human interest and concern, and is it ever possible for our will to hinder or to help our intellect in its grasp of the truth? The question is a subtle one; it is not summed up merely by inquiring into our ability to carry our beliefs over into our actions. It is not a matter of translating theory into practice as pragmatism has often been understood. It is rather a question of the "psychology of human opinion," in James's phrase, a question about the role played by the total person in the formation of belief.

Contrary to what might be supposed, James sided with David Hume against Descartes with regard to our believing in a certain class of facts. Concerning past fact — the existence of Caesar or the events going to make up the Civil War — our will is entirely powerless. We are determined by the facts and our grasp of them. Assuming that we have rational evidence both for the existence of Caesar and for the events of the Civil War, we are powerless, says James, to believe the contrary of these hypotheses. We may *say* that Caesar was not and that the Civil War did not occur, but "we are absolutely impotent to believe" these things. Our power of believing is bound down, there is no room for decision and our will has no role to play. As soon as we understand this point, we have an important clue to what James has in mind. The will to believe comes into play *only* in cases where our option is forced, live, and momentous *and our reason alone is unable to give us a final an-swer.* In short, the will to believe is legitimate only in situations of forced action — deciding whether to attempt saving a drowning person — or forced opinion — making up our minds about God and the imponderables in human experience.

James was not unaware of the view that, as rational beings, we are duty-bound to withhold assent until reason and evidence have decided the issue. But he was equally sensitive to the fact that life does not always afford us the luxury of time and indecision. Life demands that we choose in many cases before we know as we ideally should wish to, and there are times when a refusal to decide means, in fact, a deciding for one of the alternatives. Our failure to vote in an election often has the practical effect of our supporting one of the candidates against the other. James put the point in his own vivid way when he distinguished between "following truth" and "shunning error." To make the latter our only guide is to avoid decision in many cases where there is the slightest chance of going wrong and thus to cut ourselves off from the possibility of following an alternative which may turn out to be true. We come here to the heart of the matter. After showing that our will, our interests (what James called our "passional nature"), frequently do determine belief — as in a case where an individual will not even *consider* the arguments for a given view because he has already set his heart against the possibility of its being true — James asked whether there might not be some special cases in which the will to believe must operate not in a willful but in a legitimate way. His own statement of the thesis cannot be improved upon:

> Our passional nature not only lawfully may, but must, decide an option between propositions, whenever it is a genuine option that cannot by its nature be decided

on intellectual grounds; for to say, under such circumstances, "Do not decide, but leave the question open," is itself a passional decision — just like deciding yes or no — and is attended with the same risk of losing the truth.*

James's further elaboration of his thesis stands in need of considerable clarification. That he intended the will to believe to come into play in relation to moral and religious questions and in the working out of personal relations is clear, but his passionate form of exposition and his convictions about the importance of his doctrine led him to present it in a muddled way. At the risk of being charged with trying to improve upon theories one has not originally thought up, I shall set forth a neater formulation. There are three distinct cases or aspects to James's theory and failure to distinguish them has led to much confusion.

The first, and in many ways least defensible, case concerns the fundamental moral order. Since moral questions concern what is good or has worth, James concludes that they cannot be settled by sensible proof. If we do not *want* a moral order, says James, we cannot be made to believe in one by rational arguments. That we shall make moral distinctions and take them seriously is decided by our will and not our intellect. We must not suppose that James understands by "moral" some parochial list of rules; he is referring instead to fundamental judgments of worth and importance which guide our activities. If, for example, we are told that we ought to seek for truth by preferring scientific knowledge to any other, James would say that this is a fundamental valuation which cannot be proved except in an instrumental argument showing that seeking truth by preferring science leads to a goal already judged to be valuable. This is voluntarism in the extreme; it points to a valua-

* *The Will To Believe and Other Essays*, p. 11.

tional basis for all activity and is less like the believing with risk which characterizes the other two cases of the will to believe than it is like skepticism about ultimate premises.

More original and suggestive are the other aspects of the will to believe, for they show how "running ahead of the evidence" can make a contribution to experience and the gaining of new truths. One case concerns, for example, religious questions such as the reality of God, the power of love, the relations of friendship, the eternal character of perfection, and similar topics. If we resolutely refuse to consider the possibility of God's reality or of the thesis that "love never faileth" until we have antecedent rational proof, we shall be cut off from *putting ourselves in the place where* we could experience the very facts which might convince us. Propositions about love and about friendship concern facts and states of affairs which must be lived through to be understood. How shall we gain that understanding if, before we are willing to swim in the stream of experience, we demand convincing rational proof and refuse to budge one inch from our present position until we get it? Where the facts — the "cash value" of abstract ideas, as James liked to put it — are such that they can only be known when lived through, we must remain forever cut off from them or we must be willing to believe in their possibility at the outset and be willing to act in ways which would put us in the presence of them, if they are there to be found. If a man cannot conclusively decide whether to invest in a possible oil well on the basis of all of the scientific evidence available, he is in a position of having to decide (if at all) on "insufficient evidence." What would convince him? If seeing is believing, then surely nothing short of being in the presence of the oil-bearing strata would do the trick. But the strata are buried; as far as his experience is concerned the oil is in the "future." The only way in which it can become a present fact is for him to be willing to believe in the possibility of its existence and prove that willingness by seeking to put himself in the presence of the fact which would prove it to be there. When the will to believe means this, it has *no* tendency to *create* the fact whose possible existence calls it forth. If, to shift the example, love never faileth, if it can sustain us in agony, defeat, and even death, then the fact that it does so has to be directly experienced; we needed to believe in advance of the evidence that it might have this power and we had to risk ourselves in giving ourselves over to deeds which might prove it, but our willingness to believe did not create the fact. It only placed us in a position to see it.

The third and closely related case represents James's strongest claim; it is the situation in which willingness to believe in the possibility of a future fact such as might prove a proposition, and willingness to act in accordance with that belief, *is one of the factors helping to create the fact.* Here the will to believe does more than place us in a position to experience the future fact if and when it becomes present; the will to believe becomes a partial cause of the fact itself. In this case the fact apart from human consciousness altogether has no existence. The famous example of the railway coach expresses the point very well. A few highwaymen can successfully loot the train because the passengers, though brave and resourceful enough individually, cannot be sure (that is, do not exercise the will to believe) that the other passengers will support them if they resist. The bandits, by contrast, have no special need of the will to believe since they are already sure of each other's cooperation. The willingness to believe in the possibility of the future fact of resistance and the willingness to respond accordingly help to create the fact. For the fact which is their joint resistance depends for its very existence upon their joint resolve. The reluctance to act until there is "evidence" that the

action will succeed is what prevents the fact from coming.
James explored the further implications of such situations
in his defense of "psychic energy," or the theory that the
quantity of our energy for accomplishing any task is a function of our beliefs about the possibility of bringing it to pass.
Our energy in a given case has an upper and a lower bound
— we can run a mile in less than ten minutes, but not in less
than six — and our actual performance on a given day is in-
determinate in advance. One of the factors in our actual performance when we bend to the task is the willingness to believe in the possibility of running the mile in seven minutes.
James's view is that without this willingness our energy for
successfully completing the seven-minute performance is
smaller than it otherwise might be. The will to believe is not
an absolute power operating above and beyond the physical
factors in the situation; there are objective limits over which
human will has no control. But because the action is not fully
determinate until it is all finished and safely in the past, the
will to believe can be one of the conditions determining the
amount of energy we can muster while the deed is still in the
doing.

Study of the will to believe shows the important part which
religion played in James's total perspective. This topic is extensive and requires treatment in its own right. We may view
his ideas about God and the religious aspect of life as the cul-
mination of his philosophy, and discover at the same time how
characteristically American was his reinterpretation of traditional beliefs. On the one hand, James sought to find vital, experiential meaning for ancient beliefs; in so doing he gave
new insight into classical Christian notions. On the other hand,
he did much to take religion out of its mode of existence as a
particular historical faith and establish the idea that there is
a general "religious hypothesis" about nature, man, and God
which can be discovered in and through religious experience.

James's fundamental thesis is the primacy of immediate experience over doctrinal elaboration and the consequent elevation of religion above theology. James did more than any other thinker to establish the opinion that the religion of churches — what Americans call "organized religion" — is merely conventional and "second-hand." Genuine religion can be found only in the stirring of the individual spirit. As a consequence, the interpreting idea becomes secondary and religion is established as the directly felt state of the mind or heart. In order to find an empirical basis for religion, James sought to translate religious ideas such as God, conversion, salvation, guilt, into a "cash value" in experience. These ideas and the corresponding realities are what they are known as in the immediate experience of the individual. His famous study *The Varieties of Religious Experience* is a storehouse of first-hand experience, and when James came to sum up his conclusions in the final lecture of that book, he was astonished at "the amount of emotionality" in the text. The reason is simple: he chose as the original material for his analysis, diaries, letters, autobiographical episodes, and lyrical outbursts illustrative of religion in the human soul. Religion came to be interpreted not in terms of its theological and metaphysical cogency, but rather by taking into account its moral helpfulness and its success in integrating the divided self. There followed what Ernest Hocking has called the "retirement of the intellect" and general doubt of the value of rational formulations for making religion understandable or for defending its claims against critics of all sorts. James's practicalism later called forth Royce's jibe that, in addition to being useful, there is the question as to how religion can be shown to be true! James was, of course, also concerned for truth, but he approached the problem through changes actually wrought in the lives of persons, and he appeared — especially to those used to a more metaphysical approach — to be bypassing the theoretical question.

James saw religion as the awareness on the part of the individual of the present incompleteness and broken character of his life; this awareness leads to the question of a higher power which can complete life and overcome the destructive forces in it. God is interpreted as the higher power able to accomplish the transformations without which life must remain fragmented and subject to the destructive powers of guilt, moral failure, pride, and indeed all the sins of natural man. For James, God is no mere ideal order, because "he produces real effects" in the world, influencing the concrete and directly known self through the avenue of the "subliminal self" which extends beyond the bright circle of direct awareness. In characteristic American fashion James says: "We and God have business with each other"; this means that our destiny is to open ourselves to the influence of the higher order, the presence of which is always revealed in deed and effect. Religion is more than a new perspective on things, more than a passionate viewing of life in a more rosy light; it is the source of *new facts* in the form of renewed lives and changed persons. James's main objection to what he called "universalistic supernaturalism" is that in relating God or the Supernatural to the world *as a whole,* we lose the difference in particular fact. "Piecemeal" supernaturalism, James's name for his own position, means that the power which is God "makes a difference" *here* rather than *there,* and consequently comes home to us individually in a way that would be lost under any other circumstances. For James, and for most of the pragmatists, a God who makes no difference would be no God at all. Life is always a struggle and a doing; the divine life is no exception. God is known through the deed and in power; he is more than an idea or an ideal.

James sought to show the worth of religion in an age of science and skepticism by tracing religious faith back to its roots in direct experience and forward to its fruits in morality. In this sense his interpretation of religion, like his pragmatism, was essentially practical in character. In keeping with this, James minimized the importance of theological interpretations and formulated doctrine. Systematic theology and speculative philosophy he regarded as secondary; the spiritual life was for him a life of action and of felt piety.

It is curious that he should have been attracted by the young idealist Josiah Royce, because Royce was his opposite in so many ways, and especially in the interpretation of religion. The two shared concern for the life of religion, and neither would accept the skepticism and agnosticism which formed a large part of the intellectual climate of their time. But Royce differed sharply from James, not only on matters of philosophical doctrine, but over the interpretation of religious questions. Where James was interested in practical consequences, Royce was stressing the need for a comprehensive metaphysic which would fit together consistently with the fundamental Christian ideas.

Royce was convinced that religion requires philosophical and theological expression; he would not admit that religion can be a wholly practical affair. He demanded a consistent doctrine of God and a view of things which allows for a reconciliation between religion and science. At a time when religious faith was either rejected entirely or reduced to the proportions of morality, Royce spoke out in defense of the rational truth of religious doctrines. He reinterpreted ancient religious ideas in terms of his own idealist metaphysic and he refused to accept the prevalent view that the meaning of theological expressions is to be found in the conduct to which they lead. No other American philosopher was Royce's equal in synthesizing philosophy and religion.

III

Josiah Royce: THE ETERNAL, THE PRACTICAL,

AND THE BELOVED COMMUNITY

The story of Josiah Royce's life has a truly American flavor; by a slight distortion of the facts it might even be made into a melodrama about the American pattern for success. Royce's parents were originally from the East, but they journeyed West just after the first wave of adventurers headed across the plains in 1849. Unlike James, Royce was not to enjoy the advantages of life in a well-known and fairly affluent family. He was born in a small town in California which, as he liked to describe it, was but a few years older than himself. Early in his educational career he received the opportunity — made possible by a group of interested businessmen — to study in Germany. This experience not only left a deep impression on him but it fixed the main pattern of his thought. Like the great German philosophers, Royce is to be counted among the system-builders, the comprehensive thinkers, the "great knowers" in the tradition of Western philosophy; he disliked the "piece-meal" philosophy stemming from the British tradition and so much beloved by his friend and colleague William James.

After earning a Doctor's degree at the new Johns Hopkins University, Royce taught for a time in his native California before he was invited to Harvard. James, some years his senior, had been attracted by the daring of the youthful defender of idealism, and it was he who succeeded in bringing Royce to Cambridge. There Royce remained for the rest of his career, carrying on, among other activities, what came to be known as "the battle of the Absolute."

Royce was a dialectical thinker with great courage. He struggled to give his idealism a systematic logical form. He had a robust faith in the possibility of proving philosophical conclusions and he went to great lengths to enlist the support of what was then the new mathematical logic for his rational idealism. This put him in an unenviable position — a position which seems to be the lot of all who attempt to bring together what others are bent on keeping asunder. Logicians and prophets of the new logic were generally wary of Royce's all-encompassing metaphysical idealism. Even when they were pleased by his spirited defense of their labors in the face of the unconverted, their pleasure was dulled when they saw their very instrument used to force them into the arms of the Absolute. On the other side, those prepared to rejoice over Royce's idealistic conclusions were baffled by his logical and epistemological excursions; it seemed to them that the moral and religious life ought to be able to get along without support from the theory of the continuum, or the doctrine that Truth is the least upper bound of a well-ordered series. But Royce was determined, and while we may allow that there is some artificiality in his attempt to combine mathematics and God, can we successfully argue that their complete divorce at the present time is a superior solution? For in the meantime logic has tended to move along its own formalistic path, unconcerned for the concrete reality on both sides, while religious thought has set itself, like the Pharaoh with the heart of stone, not only against logic but against philosophy as well.

In style Royce's thought represents a curious combination

of the logical elaboration we associate with the academy and the rhetorical eloquence characteristic of the popular lecture platform or the pulpit. He surely required too many words to communicate his ideas and some of his best insights are buried by parenthetical commentary and unenlightening qualification. He often wrote as though he were delivering a sermon, giving his writing a didactic air that is distracting and even annoying to the reader. To get a complete picture of his philosophy one has to read both systematic works, like *The World and the Individual,* which contain well-reasoned arguments, and more popular writings such as *The Philosophy of Loyalty,* which is aimed at edifying the brethren.

The charge has often been made that Royce did not develop a philosophy indigenous to American life, but instead transported old European ideas to America, trying to give them in the process a native air. That charge as it stands is wrong, but it points to important truths about Royce's thought. He began with ideas as old as those of Plato and Aristotle and he depended upon their modern reformulations in the systems of the great German idealists, Kant and Hegel. But to this idealist tradition he gave a characteristic twist which brought it closer to American life. Whereas the classical idealists had invariably defined man in terms of his reason and his never-ending quest for knowledge of reality, Royce directed attention to the human *will.* Life is governed by plans and purposes and even reason is not beyond the guidance of the will. The individual is not distinguished so much by the truth he grasps as by the unique purpose he fulfills in the divine economy. An individual reveals himself most truly in the cause to which his will is devoted. This view earned for Royce the title of "voluntarist"; no matter how much he stressed the idea of absolute truth or the ideal of a perfect knowledge, in the end he maintained that it is the purpose embodied in our will that makes us genuine individuals.

Royce and his way of thinking finally ran counter to the main stream of American thought. Pragmatism — and not the sort of pragmatism Royce had in mind when he described himself as an "absolute pragmatist" — was destined to carry the day and the comprehensive idealism Royce represented gradually declined. The more America became aware of its destiny as a technical civilization, the more its thinkers felt the need to think in instrumentalist or "practical" terms. The demand to solve concrete and immediate problems tended to crowd out the concern for speculative and ultimate questions. When success in practice is the immediate issue, it is difficult to turn one's mind to questions about the meaning of success itself and what its worth would be if you had it.

The clue to Royce's thought is to be found in the grasp of one point: he resisted the tendency to reduce everything to the level of the immediately practical because of his conviction that, without the timeless and the Eternal, the immediately practical has little meaning and less worth. Unlike many other American thinkers, he was not afraid of the speculative flight of thought and he would not sacrifice his belief that ideas which are generally thought to be recondite and remote have an intimate bearing upon the simplest and most commonplace experience. Santayana complained that Royce wanted to prove everything by rational dialectic. This may be true, but there is a daring and a spirit of adventure in Royce's attempt to keep logic in touch with life, which is more compelling than an urbane philosophy supposed to be superior to all proof. Royce's thought is not free of an academic flavor and it has its sanctimonious air, but it is more in touch with American life than critics have been willing to acknowledge. For what could

be more characteristic of the American spirit than a philosophy
which starts with the fact of tension, struggle, opposing forces,
differences of opinion, and then seeks to mitigate the destructive consequences of these opposites by containing them in a
wider, more inclusive unity? The principle of *community*,
Royce's central philosophical idea, is intended to create one
out of many. It aims at overcoming what is divisive and preserving what is distinctive in a plurality of individuals which,
left to themselves, would exhaust each other in fruitless struggle. Whether we believe in the ultimate validity of Royce's
philosophy or not, there can be no doubt that he saw the basic
problem of the American experiment: *How is it possible to
harmonize many different and opposing wills without resort-
ing to a collectivism in which all individuals are lost?* For him
community was the answer to that question; it meant the quest
for a form of life which is beyond the twin distortions of collectivism and individualism.

Our tendency to think of community only in connection with
social, political, and religious problems must not be allowed
to obscure the very general meaning which the community
principle had in Royce's thought. The principle appears, in
one form or another, in the solution to every problem whether
in science or morality, society or religion. In every sphere difficulties are overcome through the creation of some form of
community — a loyal togetherness of many individual elements dedicated to a common goal. The conquest of error in
knowledge is accomplished by creating a community of critical
investigators for whom the pursuit of an objective truth out-
weighs all other concerns; confusion in ethics is attacked by
engendering loyalty to an overarching good; warring tendencies in society are checked by subordinating them to a common interest; guilt and the consequences of the tragic deed
are nullified through the redeeming power of the Beloved Com-

munity — the invisible unity of individuals bound together by their common devotion to the principle of Christian love.

While Royce's system has its own integrity as the answer to basic problems which he regarded as perennial in human life, it is clear that much of what is distinctive in his absolute idealism came from his protracted efforts to incorporate what he took to be true in pragmatism into his own scheme. Royce learned and developed much from a life-long dialogue with his colleague William James. Unlike the British idealists whose thought also stemmed from Hegel, Royce did not regard pragmatism as just so much error and subjective fancy. He saw in it the truth that thinking is as much an activity as anything else we do, that it is done because we need to do it, and that it is guided throughout by purposes and goals. Royce's own form of voluntarism represents not only a novel turn in the theory of absolute idealism, but it was developed partly in response to James's charge that he was a consummate rationalist. It was Royce's way of connecting theoretical knowledge with the ideals of conduct, a synthesis which he liked to call "absolute pragmatism." obj. truth + Know an purposin

Royce's major problem was the same as that of every dia- respun lectical thinker: he saw truth in each of two opposing tendencies and he had to find a way of combining these insights in a genuine synthesis of novel character. On one side, he was the heir of the great rationalist tradition, tinged as it was with the theological conception of God as the knower of all truth. From this position he derived the doctrine of an objective truth that is beyond the power of human beings to alter. On the other hand, he was sensitive to the idea that knowledge must be related to our ideals of conduct and that every judgment, far from being a passive copying of the environment, is in fact an active response to the consciousness of a need. Having accepted these conclusions, Royce's problem was to see whether they might be combined in a way which would overcome the difficulties each position must face when it is pressed to its logical limit. Royce would not go along with the thoroughgoing intellectualism of the rationalist position. Much as he liked to contemplate the timeless truth which the Absolute would possess, he could not agree in separating this truth from will and purpose. Man, he saw, is more than a knower; he is a doer as well and one who must seek to work out his salvation through fear and trembling. His voluntarism, or doctrine of purpose, at the root of all thought expressed his break with orthodox rationalism. But Royce was equally critical of much pragmatist talk about truth being made, about knowledge being a matter of our success in meeting our needs; he was uneasy in the face of a philosophy which seemed to place usefulness ahead of truth. Against all this he argued that pragmatism, though it harbors an important truth in itself, cannot be regarded as true in its own terms. The total truth, could we achieve it, would be a synthesis of absolutism and pragmatism — "absolute pragmatism."

It would be merely pedantic to engage in a comparison between Royce's version of what pragmatism means and the pronouncements of its avowed representatives such as James and Dewey. No critic ever suceeds in giving a fully sympathetic interpretation of a position which he finds ultimately unsatisfactory; Royce was no exception. Dewey later read Royce out of the pragmatist camp, claiming that his voluntarism differed from pragmatic doctrine in important points. Royce did, however, take the statements of James very seriously and it was with these pronouncements that he occupied himself and against which he reacted. More important than deciding about matters of academic influences is some understanding of what Royce believed to be true in pragmatism. For despite his criticisms of the pragmatist outlook he stoutly defended it against the various realisms and copy theories of knowledge and he was ever ready to defend the claim that a truth unconnected with human purpose is no truth at all.

Royce's "practicalism," if we may use the term to avoid confusion, started with the idea that all human activity represents some response to the environment and is an expression of the individual self. Like the pragmatists, he rejected the ancient theory of knowledge as the passive reception and copy of a previously given and independent reality. Knowledge means judgment and judgment is an active response. All thought is, in the first instance, activity. We approach the world as creatures of many purposes and needs. Life demands both the fulfilling of the needs and expressing of the purposes. Success is, Royce would admit, a matter of adjustments and it requires an active, constructive response by the human subject. If there were no interest in knowing things and no need to do so, man would never have developed a body of knowledge in the first place. In holding these views, Royce believed that he was giving voice to genuinely pragmatist theses. But there was a problem about pragmatism which Royce could never solve and it represents a difficulty singled out by many others as well. James often spoke as though there were a necessary connection between what we *need* to believe on a particular occasion and the truth of that belief. Put in this way the doctrine appeared to Royce as willful subjectivism in which the need of the moment is invested with a normative character it does not deserve to have. For Royce, the claim to truth, though it arises out of a concrete situation involving human needs and interests, cannot be divorced from *constraining grounds* which take us beyond the needs of any individual and the demands of any particular situation.

It is at this point, and without further inquiry into the details of pragmatist doctrine, that Royce inserts the condition

which is characteristic of his entire philosophy. In making the
claim that a given belief is true we cannot be saying that the
belief is true only for the person who utters it and only for the
moment at which the claim is made. Royce's point is that truth,
though it be defined in terms of individual needs and adjustments, cannot be limited to the need of *this* individual at *that*
moment because it is essential to the idea of truth that it be
binding upon all selves at *all* moments. A transcendence, in
other words, of the single moment in time and of the isolated
singular individual has to be made. Using the language of
pragmatism, Royce held that the *need* of the moment at which
a truth is proclaimed is to be judged by or to be under the
control of other moments which, though different from it, have
something in common at the same time. He was fond of pointing out that when pragmatists claim truth for their view and
say that it ought to be believed in contrast to other alternative views of the nature of truth and of knowledge, they are
going far beyond the fulfillment of any individual need or adjustment to the environment. They are in effect laying down
a pattern determining a standard need, a need for all men
who seek truth and who can distinguish between a merely
physical reaction and critical judgment. When the claim of
the moment is the truth of what is said at that moment, then
the moment is legislating for all other moments. The moment,
if it understood itself, its plan, its intention, would become
conscious of going far beyond itself. For Royce the problem
of truth is how the claim of the moment can be transformed
from a mere brute fact — the fact of this individual at this
moment fulfilling his need — into a judgment which has behind it the warrant of many critical moments. The reference
to the other moments brings in the social principle.

Royce saw that knowledge always means *criticism*. Knowledge is never the acquiesence in a claim made at one moment

in time by one individual, but rather bringing the critical force of other moments to bear upon a claim to truth in the effort to escape insularity and idiosyncrasy. Just as we need to check on ourselves and our opinions by finding the companion who sees the reality as we do, so the need of the moment is to find confirmation in other moments. Corroboration means a plurality of witnesses testifying to the same fact. Royce was ready to express the principle in terms of human need. The expression of a present need can legitimately be called true only if something more than the expression of the present need is acknowledged. The something more is the further need to believe that the present need is as it *ought* to be — a need, that is, which others also may have and ought to have if they are also seekers after truth. The absolute character of Royce's practicalism consists in making the need *universal*, a standard for all men. In appealing to a universal standard Royce remained faithful to his idealism. It was more usual for the critics of pragmatism to claim that the object of ordinary experience is utterly *independent* of all human faculties and that to gain truth we need but to copy that object. Royce's idealism precluded that sort of appeal. Instead he went along with the doctrine that knowledge is the expression of a need and a constructive response to the environment, hoping to answer the charge of subjectivism by introducing among our needs the need to appeal to other experience as the basis of objective truth. A judgment which meets the latter need has a basis in truth. But then it is no private expression of an inner need of one individual adjusting himself to the environment; it is a critical consensus involving the control of the original judgment by many others. Royce's so-called absolutism was the attempt to find a basis for truth, not by confronting the pragmatist with the old realism — completed objects which we passively copy — but by universalizing the character of man's response to his world. When we express what we need to acknowledge, and make the claim that our judgment is true, we must go on to understand the full meaning of our claim. We must understand that what we really mean in making the claim to truth is that all men under the same circumstances would have the same need and would express it in the same way.

Royce was fond of expressing his idea of the social principle in knowledge by referring to the development of science. An individual investigator, for example, finds himself led to acknowledge certain facts. Let these facts be the records of the behavior of certain gases under well-defined conditions. The investigator sets forth his results in the form of numerical tables correlating the volume, pressure, and temperature of the gases such that a definite pattern is discernible in the relations of the numbers. He then formulates this pattern as a law of behavior governing certain natural objects and claims that we have new scientific truth. The first point, says Royce, is that we do not forthwith write these results down in the book of science as if the investigator had said, "Lo, I have made a discovery and a new truth." The published result represents a judgment and a claim to truth, but thus far the claim does not extend beyond the experience of the investigator. To provide rational grounds for the claim we must show that it is valid beyond the moment and that it is not confined to the experience of but one individual. The behavior of the natural objects in question must be capable of reproduction in the experience of others. The original judgment made by one self at one moment is subjected to other judgments made by others at other moments. Successful corroboration means that the relevant experience of other selves yields the same result as that expressed in the original claim to discovery. Science thus presupposes and rests upon a community of knowers, whose

aim is the discovery of truth; an individual claim to truth
merits the status of knowledge only when it fulfills the demand put upon it by that community.

Despite the large emphasis placed by Royce on the theory
of knowledge, it would be an error to suppose that his thought
is no more than a complex epistemological theory. More important by far is his treatment of moral and religious issues,
especially the idea of loyalty as both a principle and a passion
which unites many distinct selves in a community. Royce's
whole philosophy could be interpreted as the story of the co-
operation and tension between individual and community. He
was sensitive to the evil tendencies in each as well as to the
value of their ideal forms. Though he always upheld the importance of the individual, his freedom and uniqueness as a
creature who is no mere interchangeable part in a vast mechanism, he was also aware of the destructive tendencies of *individualism* and the refusal to acknowledge the need for co-
operation. On the other hand, while Royce sang the praises
of true community as the most powerful civilizing force in
human life, he was not unmindful of the evils of that degenerate form of community which expresses itself most violently
in the form of the "mob" and less obtrusively, though no less
destructively, in the form of mere social conformity. True
community does not mean an impersonal mass; true individuality does not mean a willful person who, in the drive to
realize himself and have his way, becomes the sworn enemy
of social co-operation. In ideal terms the two belong together,
but under the conditions of human life as we know it there
is a tension between them. The problem is their reconciliation.

In order to see how Royce believed it possible to show the
intimate relation between concrete human life and activity on
the one hand and that form of the Eternal which he generally
called the Absolute on the other, it is necessary to penetrate

the mystery of the community idea. Though Royce, reviewing the development of his thought later in life, overestimated the role played by the idea of the community in his thinking, there is no doubt that it furnishes the key to much of his philosophical message. In Royce's view all the genuine forms of community both express and rest upon an ideal order which is never fully realized in the experience of any individual or in any finite collection of individuals. The divine life is realized in and through individuals as members of communities, the goals of which — called by Royce their "causes" — define certain ideal fulfillments. The scientific community, for example, is devoted to the pursuit of a truth which is the possession of no mortal, and its goal is a unity of knowledge and understanding that transcends our present life. The religious community, also known as the Beloved Community, is a unity of charity and insight which has the power to redeem human failure and link many selves together in a life which both fulfills and passes beyond them at the same time. The goals of the communities express the life of the Absolute Self.

Royce made a serious attempt to analyze the nature of community in precise terms and his studies reflect researches then being carried on in the fields of social psychology and anthropology. Community, as an identifiable form of life, is to be found wherever three conditions are fulfilled. There must first be a plurality of individual selves, aware of their own identity as individual persons and capable of viewing themselves as beings extending over time. Unlike many other rationalist thinkers, Royce did not view the self as a given *substance* which is a present and finished datum to be captured in the spotlight of the inward gaze. The self is what Royce called an "interpretation," that is, a center of meaning which is neither a datum for sense nor a universal to be grasped by reason. His doctrine of the self is as original as it is difficult to follow. The main point is that every individual has some part in determining how much of the past will enter into the ideal meaning of his life. That I thus interpret myself is the fact which expresses my freedom to decide, within limits, what I shall identify myself with and what I shall set aside as having no part in my being.

In the second place, the ideally extensible selves must be seen as genuinely distinct beings. The point is an important one and Royce was often the victim of misunderstanding in regard to it. Community never meant a blending of selves, a merging into one another in mystical fashion. There can be no community without distinct selves because it is a living unity of diverse individuals and not a mass in which all are swallowed up. We need not go into the intricacies of the theory of individuality; it points to an ancient problem and Royce had his own complex solution to it. One point, however, is essential; and it reveals the strongly American character of his thought. The distinctness of selves is most vivid neither in feeling nor in taking thought, but in decision and in action. Royce believed that we are most aware and sure of our individuality and uniqueness when we are called upon to choose a plan of action, to act, and then to accept the responsibility for what we have done. We are most aware of being unique and distinct from all other selves when we are called on to act. Our ideas might be held in common with another, and the bonds of sympathy might become so strong that one consciousness would feel in concert with another, but when it comes to the deed, each of us is alone and knows that he is alone. In Royce's world there are real individuals; without them there can be no community.

The third condition was regarded by Royce as by far the most important. A community exists when many distinct selves, each capable of viewing themselves as creatures extending

over a period of time, can come to acknowledge certain deeds
and events of the past and certain anticipated goals in the
future as their own. The shared element brings the members
together in a genuine unity because each member, though distinct in his own consciousness and freedom, still identifies himself with the same past events and future hopes which form
a part of the reality of all the other selves. Just as a community
describes one of its heroes not merely as *a* hero but as *our* hero,
so the individual members know themselves to be bound together when they realize that some of the facts they identify
themselves with are also accepted by all the other selves as
defining their identity. Royce saw that some communities are
oriented to the past in an especially powerful way; they can
be called "communities of memory." Others find their binding
element in hoped-for events in the future; they are "communities of hope." In view of the fact that a community, being a
form of life, must exist in time, every community will share
both the common past or memory and the common future or
hope, but the emphasis will differ under differing circumstances and some communities will come to be identified as
predominantly one or the other. A labor union, for example,
as a special form of community is more likely to be a community of hope, orienting itself toward certain hoped-for goals.
Patriotic organizations, on the other hand, are largely communities of memory, since they draw their inspiration from
the events of bygone days and in some instances exist primarily
for preserving the past unchanged.

When the nature of community is stated in this analytical
way it may appear that we have no more than a tissue of ideas
devoid of concrete embodiment and life. This is not so. Community is a definite, historical form of life. It depends, to be
sure, upon common understanding among the members, but
it rests even more upon a passionate virtue which moves them

to action while it binds them together in devotion. This virtue
is *loyalty*. Royce sought to disengage loyalty from its exclusively civic and martial setting, claiming that its range is universal. Whenever diverse individuals are ready to devote themselves to a common purpose — a goal or cause, as he called it
— they are bound together at the same time by a common
loyalty. Such devotion in loyalty, moreover, is more than a
feeling existing within the inner recesses of the mind; it is
an active giving of the self to a larger life and it must express
itself in concrete deeds. The individual in devoting himself to
the cause is committed to the performance of concrete acts
that have a definite relevance to the cause of the community
and help to realize the purpose for which it exists. A member
does not fulfill his role if he does no more than feel or profess
an abstract loyalty to or sympathy for the goal; the deed is required as the outward expression of the loyal spirit. In this way
a community, though it is heavily dependent upon the ideal
spirit of understanding, takes on concrete existence in a world
of time and change. It lives in and through the efforts of its
members to realize the cause for which the community exists.

In reply to the charge that a community engulfs the individual and stifles his individuality, Royce asked that we bear
two things in mind. First, the individual expresses his freedom
in the act of joining the community; he is not compelled to do
so by forces outside himself. The point of stressing our ability
to extend ourselves ideally in time and thus to decide what
belongs to us and what does not is to call attention to our freedom. There is no loyalty which is not a *willing* devotion to the
cause. Secondly, Royce insisted upon a distinction between
a community and a crowd or "mob." The distinction is basic
and it shows his deep insight into the problems of social life.
The mob spirit — whether it exists in the immediate form of
a surging mass ready to take the law into its own hands, or

in the more subtle form of mass opinion stampeded into conformity by the demagogue, the popular commentator, or the
advertiser — is an uncritical spirit; it is a largely unintelligent
spirit based upon sympathy and the desire of the individual
to sacrifice himself, his ideas, his critical acumen, in order to
rid himself of his individual responsibility. Unlike many philosophers who have spoken uncritically about an ethics of sympathy, Royce saw that sympathy all by itself is blind. We can
sympathize with anything, with the tyrant bent on cruelty and
oppression as well as with the doctor devoted to the alleviation
of human suffering. Sympathy, as mere enthusiasm to "feel
with" the others, to join them by giving up ourselves, is more
like a hypnotic response than a critical one. A mob is not a
community chiefly because the latter can exist only through
the intelligent loyalty of its members. For the community to
succeed it needs the benefit of the forethought and criticism
of its members; in devoting themselves to the cause they do
not thereby give up their minds and their senses. The mob,
on the contrary, is made up of individuals who have sacrificed
these powers; in sympathizing with the man whose voice or
personality or whose prejudices hypnotize them and deprive
them of their reason, they are losing themselves in that sort
of sacrifice which has no final purpose. The members of the
genuine community are losing their lives in order to find them.
Through the doctrine of the community Royce introduced
his idea of the Eternal, the time-transcending standpoint from
which he criticized the excessive practicalism of the American
mind. If, he argued, human life is to be understood as a drive
toward fulfillment or, in more familiar terms, *success*, the most
important question we can ask is: What is success and how
shall we know when we have it? Royce saw that, despite everything that had been said about the "crassness" and "material-
ism" of American pragmatic thinking, underneath it all lay

the idea of purpose; present life is interpreted and justified through its contribution to the future. Royce's concern was that we be self-conscious and understand what this means. The idea of success all by itself is vague enough, and despite its magic, it provides little guidance unless we have given thought to what we want, what it means to succeed. Let self-fulfillment or success be the goal; what self shall we realize? Which one is our real self? In putting these questions, Royce gave expression to what he called the will to be self-possessed. It seemed to him that if the individual is to avoid wasting his life in an endless round of largely trivial activities he must have some clear idea of himself and his purpose which goes beyond the immediate moment. He must come to believe that beyond his self of the present there is a larger or ideal self which, if brought to realization, would represent his real being and place in the scheme of things. Royce saw that the older religious belief in a purposive order, in which each individual had a place that could be filled by no other, had decayed. Gone was a sense of individual purpose and destiny to be fulfilled by an enduring self. Instead the goal of immediate success defined by the pleasure, the whim, or the fancy of the momentary self had taken command. Not only was the larger self neglected, the self defined by lasting goals able to withstand the corrosive effects of evil and tragedy, but the very idea of such a self had died. Royce did not try to submerge the individual in society as has often been held; on the contrary, he saw that belief in the individual had been lost precisely because men no longer believed in an ideal order which provides an ultimate purpose for each individual by holding out a place to be filled by him alone and by no other individual. The real self, the larger or enduring self is known through that ideal order; it is, in short, defined through its ultimate destiny or purpose. Historians of thought have called this view an idealist version of Old fashioned Calvinism. Will See 101 an idealist version of old-fashioned Calvinism; it would be more accurate to describe it as Royce's interpretation of Christianity.

Royce first worked out his theory of the Absolute and of our necessary involvement in the life of an Eternal consciousness in connection with his theory of knowledge. In a well-known discussion called "The Possibility of Error" he had tried to show that appeal to an absolute knower is logically involved in a normative definition of truth. In an argument now famous for its daring, Royce claimed that it is impossible to define what we mean by an error unless we refer, at least intentionally, to an ideal truth known to a consciousness out of time. An error, to be real, must be about a real being and it must stand in contrast to a real truth about that being. The real being and the real truth are not actually possessed by any finite being in time, but both are intended by such beings. The will to truth, properly understood, is the will to possess a system of completed knowledge about a real being. But if we intend without possessing the truth, we must be aiming at a completed consciousness which, though actual, is not fully realized for any single individual. The object of our will, our goal or cause, is thus an ideal limit which gives point to our present activity. Our search for the truth, our willingness to discipline ourselves in order to realize our will to truth, has a purpose *at the present moment* if the ideal at which we aim has a reality of its own and is no mere human fancy or whim. This is the crucial point; a human activity which aims at a critical result meant to be binding upon human intelligence cannot have for its end or goal a mere projection or construction of the human will. A critical result demands a standard constraining individual willfulness; a goal which human beings completely control through their own will is inadequate to this demand. Either activity aiming at a critical result is pointless and illusory, or its goal is a superhuman and supertemporal reality which can be discovered only through disciplined effort. When Royce described purposive activity as "seeking a city out of sight," he meant to express the superhuman character of the goal, both in the sense that it is not now possessed by any finite being and that it is not a construction or projection of the human will.

If we look at this seemingly abstruse analysis more closely, we see that it is actually an expression of the community principle all over again. The pursuit of knowledge is a quest carried on by many beings, each of whom freely acknowledges an ideal goal and conscientiously devotes his energies to, and allows his activity to be guided by, the cause for which the community exists. All the members are bound together by their acknowledgment of the common cause and all are loyal to it. The scientific community, of course, realizes its members only to the extent that they are pursuers of theoretical and abstract truth; insofar as human beings have other aims and interests they will have to give themselves to other communities. But these communities will have the same general structure; they will embody a corporate life in which many distinct members are unified through their loyalty to the pursuit of a common goal. The validity of their quest as a body depends upon the reality of their cause; the purposive nature of their individual lives depends upon the contribution which they make to the realization of this cause. Each individual discovers his larger self through the sacrifice of his own willfulness, prejudice, and caprice. The presence of the Eternal in the practical coincides with our conscious grasp of the larger self. Wherever two or three are gathered together — Royce was fond of paraphrasing biblical passages — for the purpose of pursuing a goal, a community exists and individual life has added a new dimension to it. In devoting themselves to the cause, the members willingly agree, each in concert with the others, to perform whatever deeds are necessary for achieving the goal and to refrain from such willful self-assertion as would harm the cause. They lose their lives in service in order to find them in a purpose for life. The Eternal is the sustaining force of all community and the condition for true selfhood at the same time.

The concept of the time-transcending purpose or cause at the foundation of the community furnished Royce with the necessary means for interpreting religion and morality in critical terms. He persistently maintained that neither the norm of conduct nor the concepts of God and religion can be clearly understood without a general theory of the nature of things. Philosophical reflection and criticism lie at the roots of the good life in all its aspects. To understand the connection between Royce's practicalism and the idea of the Absolute we need to see how the community doctrine enters into the major problem of ethics and how the special form of community known as the Beloved Community represents the solution to the religious problem. In each case concrete human experience is endowed with a new meaning through the discovery of its involvement with the Absolute, or time-spanning consciousness.

Royce saw the fundamental problem of ethics as one of combining two elements in polar tension with each other. On the one side there is the principle of self-direction or, in the language of Kant, the *autonomy* of the will. When we face the question of our duty, and the reason which can be given for regarding an action as right or obligatory, we come finally to our own will. For a being with freedom, no external authority can be the ultimate ground of action. "My duty," said Royce, "is simply my own will brought to my clear self-consciousness." On the other side, however, stands a second prin-

ciple which is no less necessary to a proper understanding of
the ethical problem. I am unable to discover what my will
is merely by introspection because I am a creature of multiple
interests and momentary desires; in variety I see no clear
standard or guide, and from momentary desires I derive what
is but a fragment of myself, which may change and thus deceive me. If the first principle is valid and I am finally to return to my own will as the source of authority, the second
principle poses the question What is my will? and answers
by pointing out the impossibility of discovering that will by
consulting myself alone. Stated in the form of a paradox, the
problem is clear enough; my own reasonable will alone can
tell me *why* something is my duty, but by remaining solely
within my own private consciousness I cannot know *what* my
will is. In one of his succinct summaries Royce says:

> Here, then, is the paradox. I, and only I, whenever I
> come to my own, can morally justify to myself my own
> plan of life. No outer authority can ever give me the
> true reason for my duty. Yet I, left to myself, can never
> find a plan of life. I have no inborn ideal naturally pres-
> ent within myself. By nature I simply go on crying out
> in a sort of chaotic self-will, according as the momen-
> tary play of desire determines.*

Royce's solution for the paradox is ultimately bound up with
the idea of the community, but it is also dependent upon his
theory of self-consciousness. We need not dwell on the com-
plexities of the latter; one essential point will suffice. Influenced by certain facts brought forth by the then novel science
of social psychology, Royce attacked the classical theory that
self-consciousness is achieved through the medium of introspection and self-analysis. As against the intuitive view, he
advanced the idea that each of us comes to a knowledge of

* *Philosophy of Loyalty,* p. 31.

himself through a process of comparison and imitation involving other selves. Self-consciousness is not an achievement of an isolated individual; it is a *social* affair to which other selves contribute. Robinson Crusoe might learn some external facts about himself — that he was not as tall as a palm tree, for example — without the help of another human creature, but he could not discover his attitudes, the tendencies of his heart, the plan of his life, confined only to his own consciousness and cut off from intercourse with other human beings. Other selves act, as it were, like mirrors in which we come to discover who and what we are.

In considering the ethical problem Royce was carrying the analysis one step further. Social intercourse, especially our power of learning through imitation, not only brings us to self-awareness, but it fills us with the variety of interests, desires, tendencies, and plans which make it difficult for us to chart a clear course and find ourselves as unified beings. At first we view ourselves with the assurance that we are unified and self-contained. Our dealings with others bring the awareness that we are far otherwise. We become conscious of the many potential selves within us, and our assurance is shaken because we now have the problem of deciding which self we shall try to become. If we are driven from our isolation in order to achieve self-knowledge, the source of our knowledge about our life-plan must also come from outside our private consciousness. This is the conclusion Royce wanted. Though we retain freedom in carrying out our will, knowledge of that will must come from beyond our own horizon. To decide who we are and what we shall become it is not enough merely to consult our private consciousness. We are to look instead to the world around us and see what work lies there waiting for us to do.

Loyalty as a virtue loomed large in Royce's view because he

saw in it, and in the communities to which its spirit gives birth, the possibility of overcoming the tension between the two aspects of the moral situation. A form of life had to be found which would make room for the individual will and its authority on the one hand, and for its concrete content on the other. Loyalty to a community combines both; the individual gives himself in a *willing* devotion, for genuine loyalty cannot be compelled from without. But in so devoting himself to a cause shared by many people, the individual finds a plan and purpose for his life which he could not have discovered by remaining within the confines of his own consciousness. Since loyalty has many forms — domestic, professional, commercial, religious, political — the loyal individual will find himself at once a member of many communities devoted to many causes. One of the major problems of the person is to find that overarching cause which will serve to put some order in his many loyalties; the unity of the self demands a unity in loyalties.

Royce was acutely aware of a basic problem in American life which loomed large in his own time and remains with us in ours. His views on the problem have given rise to needless misunderstanding. The problem is this: Since America was founded on a belief in individual freedom and the right of the person to self-determination, how can a form of life be developed which will do justice to both the belief and the right *at the same time* that there is sufficient acknowledgment of social life and of the common good to permit the development of a national unity? Royce defended the individual and his right of self-determination throughout his life, but he vigorously attacked and rejected *individualism*. The distinction is fundamental. He knew well enough that no man is an island, that human life has a social dimension which is no mere illusion or necessary evil. It seemed to him that an irresponsible individualism must finally lead to a state of chaos in which individual rights themselves will disappear. This is, of course, an old problem, and Royce saw the special form in which it presented itself upon the American scene. Train a man to self-assertion and, though there is a undying truth in such asser-tion, if he has no other training the result can be nothing but the death of the commonwealth. Can there be a respect for a development of individual freedom which is at the same time filled with a sense of obligation to social order? This was Royce's question, put to himself and to his contemporaries. His answer was in the doctrine of community, a unity of in-dividual freedom and social co-operation. When he attacked individualism, he was making no assault on the individual; he was merely trying to recover an old truth. Where there is no social order, neither is there acknowledgment of individual rights. Where every individual views the world and other selves as no more than an unlimited field for self-assertion, the time must come when even that willfulness itself is no longer possible. In rejecting individualism Royce was not re-jecting the individual; he was trying instead to point out that where no community exists, no individual self-development can exist either. *Universal Loyalty to loyalty*

In a typically ingenious fashion, Royce tried to give to his doctrine of loyalty a universal form so that it might take its place with such ethical principles as Kant's categorical im-perative or Mill's principle of utility. Consequently he de-vised the formula of "loyalty to Loyalty." Like many universal principles, this one appears empty and vague, and in addition it seems to suffer from a redundancy on its very face. We need not argue that it furnishes a final solution to the ethical prob-lem in order to see the element of truth in it. Our guide in life is this: Choose your cause and serve it so that, through your choice and your service, loyalty will be extended and increased among men. The identical terms in the formula actually differ in meaning. The individual is asked to be loyal; this is the first loyalty. He is asked to show this in a concrete form through some particular form of co-operation. Through his choice and devotion he advances the specific cause of the community to which he belongs; his community in turn extends the scope and power of loyalty among men. This is the second loyalty. If the objection be raised, as it was in Royce's time, that there are evil communities, that for example, a band of swindlers or assassins must exhibit loyalty in order to exist and carry out their aims, the reply is that they are loyal but *not* to loyalty. Their efforts do not extend the loyal spirit among men since they are engaged in destruction and in sowing suspicion and hatred. Insofar as they have a community at all, they must exhibit some loyalty, but insofar as their cause does not extend the loyal spirit it is an evil cause and fails to meet the demand of the principle.

Many of the communities to which we belong are limited in scope and succeed in realizing their causes within the lifetime of most if not all of their members. But there are other communities devoted to certain causes which are so far reaching in scope and so difficult of achievement that they are never realized within the life of any member or collection of members. These communities, dedicated to transcendent ideals, represent the ideal aspects of life; the pursuit of beauty, of knowledge, of peace, of God. The ideal of a community of all mankind — sometimes called by Royce the Great Community — is found in the scientific community, dedicated to the discovery of a truth which is austere and beyond the special interests and prejudices of any man or group; and in the religious community aiming at the unity of the brethren in God and at the recovery of the individual from his own willfulness, his deeds of disloyalty, and the burden of failures for which he cannot forgive himself. These communities seek, in the truest sense, what

Royce called "the city out of sight." These causes are such that, in principle, no individual will experience in his own life their final realization. Viewed as goals to be reached through a series of acts, the process appears indeed as an infinite one. Moreover, the movement toward the goal is no uninterrupted or unimpeded advance; there are powers of evil as well. In place of truth we believe much error; instead of loyalty we find disloyalty; though we seek peace and co-operation we perpetrate conflict and insist upon having our own way; we lose God and find only doubt and despair in his place. These transcending causes, then, are not only beyond the possibility of our directly verifying their success, but they are threatened with another and more terrifying possibility, the possibility of being *lost* causes. Royce posed the question of the lost cause by asking about its implications for the individual. Can a person find self-realization through choosing and serving a lost cause, a cause which is doomed never to be realized?

Royce's answer to his own question discloses the heart of his idealism. To the Absolute or time-spanning consciousness, a cause may be real which has no worldly fulfillment; individuals may find their own realization through service to such causes if they can understand why their cause cannot be realized in some earthly state of affairs. Royce's idea is that the true nature of spiritual fulfillment comes home to us when we discover ourselves devoted to a cause whose fulfillment cannot be equated with events within human history. The concrete illustrations which clarify this point serve at the same time to disclose the intimate connection between loyalty and religion, which comes to its fullest expression in the idea of the Beloved Community. The continuing religious communities which form the basis of the Old and New Testaments include the experience of the lost cause within their own lives. Although in both cases we find that a close relationship is maintained between faith in God and historical life, there is a common discovery of the impossibility of identifying the goal of the community with a wholly historical state of affairs. In the Hebraic community the prophetic tradition had gradually come to maintain that the ideal community of those who love the Lord and walk in peace with each other cannot be understood after the fashion of an historical kingdom. The goal of the divine government of the world is a "city out of sight"; it lives in the vision of those who love it and are loyal to it, but it is more than a human kingdom. It is a kingdom or community of those who have, as the prophet Jeremiah expressed it, the law written in their inward parts; it transcends the historical horizon in its fullness. Those who expect the realization of this community in history are doomed to regard their cause as a "lost" cause, but its being lost to the world does not mean that it is lost in every sense. For it may have a new type of being, a being which goes beyond the temporal; thus is born the idea of a divine kingdom.

The New Testament represents a similar development within the lives of those who followed Jesus as the expected Messiah. That the ideal of the Kingdom of God was first taken by these followers to be an historical community is well known to all students of early Christianity. The disappointment of their hopes brought on one of the major crises in the history of the Christian church. They had to make a momentous decision. If the cause — the Kingdom of God — to which they had given their lives was but one more earthly kingdom, then they had devoted themselves to an illusion. But suppose the Kingdom is a "lost" cause, only in the sense that it cannot be realized as one more earthly kingdom in the world as we know it. What follows from this supposition? The answer given by the New Testament communities was that the ideal community, the Kingdom of God, is a spiritual unity of persons in God which

transcends history. The experience of the lost cause gives rise
to the faith that the cause is real in another order of being;
it has power for and relevance to this world, but it is not one
more earthly kingdom in history. For God the Kingdom is a
reality; for human beings it is a reality in faith and loyalty.
It is lost to the world because the world is too small to accommodate it, but it is not lost to God. The loyal have discovered its true meaning by discovering why it is lost in the
world.

Despite the criticism of those who dismissed Royce's ideas
as no more than a substitute faith, his grasp of basic Christian
doctrines was profound and he avoided mistakes which many
theologians in his time were making. It is remarkable that at
a time when religion was reduced on all sides to morality and
good works, Royce rejected the identification, vigorously main-
taining that there are problems in human life not to be solved
by a moral idealism. There was moreover, especially in liberal
Protestantism, a marked tendency to set aside as no longer
meaningful some of the "theological" concepts of the Christian
tradition such as sin, atonement, redemption. Royce tried to
find meaning for these notions in human experience and his
attempt to show, through an interpretation of the ancient story
of Joseph and his brothers, the need for a concept of atonement in the most ordinary human life is good evidence of his
refusal to avoid difficult theological questions. While many of
his contemporaries sought to purge classical Christianity of
those elements which gave offence to the modern mind, Royce
sought to reinterpret ancient ideas in the light of current experience. He struggled to point out the perennial importance
of these ideas and he was unwilling to set them aside as
expendable merely because they had temporarily lost their
meaning.

Royce's reinterpretation of the church as the Beloved Com-

Christianly

munity combines several ideas at once. Loyalty receives a new
dimension in becoming love or charity and, as the basis of that
special community which is the redeeming community, it helps
us to understand the puzzling notion of atonement. For Royce,
atonement means the loving deed which makes it possible to
re-establish the community of love on the far side of sin and
disloyalty. In giving Himself for the founding of the Beloved
Community, Jesus performs the deed for which he is called the
Christ. Royce saw, as Matthew Arnold did not, that if the traditional doctrine of sin means no more than a morbid sense
of inadequacy or moral failure, it has lost its peculiar *religious*
meaning of separation from the divine. And if sin has no
meaning in religious terms, atonement must also lose its significance, with the result that we can no longer understand
what is meant when Jesus is called "Messiah" or "Christ." *Nice*
Royce understood all this and he tried to connect the doctrine
of sin with that of atonement. Sin he interpreted as the guilt
that stems from the knowledge of having been disloyal to the
ideal of love. It is more than transgression or the breaking of
the law; it is the guilt which follows our knowing that we
have broken the community. The disloyal deed done, or the
loyal deed left undone, plunges the self into what Royce called
the "hell of the irrevocable." Disloyalty stands as a brute fact,
a fact which no amount of taking thought will obliterate.
As Royce perceived, it does no good to counsel us, as Arnold
did, to thrust the thought of our disloyalty from us, because
this is just what we are unable to do. The brothers of Joseph
in the biblical story had broken their community of trust and
loyalty by selling him into captivity; over the years they could
not forget their treacherous deed and they feared to see his
face. The religious problem is to find a way of overcoming the
tragic consequences, for the community no less than for the
individual, of the act of disloyalty. Atonement means the

power to overcome these consequences, to destroy the hell of the irrevocable, and to re-establish the community. But if the individual cannot forgive himself and bring the reconciliation about through his own unaided will, how shall it be accomplished? Royce's answer is that it can be accomplished only through the sacrificial love which finds expression in the Christian doctrine of atonement.

Royce was unwilling to repeat old formulas. In seeking to reinterpret the idea of atonement, he rejected two extreme positions which had been developed in the course of reflection on this central topic. And in so doing he set forth the conditions which a valid account of atonement must satisfy. The sinner must be reconciled both to himself and to God; justice must be done to both aspects of the situation. There must be an actual change in the concrete or objective situation. The irrevocable deed must be transformed in some way; a change in the consciousness of the sinner alone will not suffice. Nor is it adequate to think of atonement as a cosmic transaction between divine and demonic powers taking place independently of the individual consciousness of the sinner, for the sinner must be reconciled to himself. Consequently, Royce could not accept the traditional penal theory according to which someone who *substitutes* for the sinner is sacrificed to an angry God. This view may meet the condition of an objective transformation, but it cannot reconcile the sinner to himself. Royce found the so-called moral theory equally inadequate. According to that view, repentance is the appropriate response and it is the necessary consequence of loving Jesus and wanting to imitate his ways. While this interpretation shows how the consciousness of the individual is changed, it has nothing to say about the irrevocable deed. Some way must be found which combines objective and subjective features. The idea of the Beloved Community, established by One who first caught the vision of its possibility and had the power to bring it into existence, is Royce's solution.

The Beloved Community is the unity of those who follow after Christ in love; it has the power to reconcile and redeem because it has within it the Spirit of God. Royce was well aware of the traditional doctrine of the church as the Body of Christ; he adopted this view, but he brought the doctrine of the Spirit into play in order to express the manner in which Christ is present. The religious community is the one which must provide the individual sinner with the means of overcoming his separation from God and from himself at the same time. For Royce both are to be accomplished only through a community, that is, in social terms. But that community does not come into existence simply by nature; it must be born in and of the Spirit. Jesus, in the form of the Suffering Servant, through his own love and giving of himself, establishes the redeeming community. No mere man could do this; Jesus performed the deed with the power of the divine Spirit. But it is not merely his earthly life and words which go to make up his being; it is his total life and death. He gives himself in order that the Beloved Community may be born; he lives within it as its animating Spirit. The church is not only the Body, but the Spirit as well; the full truth of Christianity must be sought in that extension of the divine life which is to be found only in the Beloved Community.

In establishing the community which no man can create by will, Jesus was making possible the looked-for atonement. The tragic past of the transgressor is not literally undone for it remains a finished fact even within the divine memory, but its meaning is no longer what it was. The Suffering Servant can bring out of the tragic past a new life, a life which would have been neither possible nor necessary without the tragic deeds giving rise to the problem of atonement in the first place. The One who is able to bring the Beloved Community into existence also creates at the same time a form of life which lays the foundation for reconciliation. Through loyalty to the Beloved Community and dedication to its cause, the individual can become reconciled to himself and to the Lord of life from whom his disloyalty has separated him.

More striking than Royce's interpretation of Christianity is the sort of enterprise it represents. It marks an undertaking possible only within the framework of American religious pluralism and freedom of religious thought. James had already begun the trend toward empiricism in religion. He had sought to revitalize religion by tracing it back to its vital source in individual experience. Ideas couched in traditional language such as salvation, being twice born, sin and others, were taken out of their fixed positions in official systems of theology and given an experiential meaning. Although James was the pioneer, Royce was even more daring in pressing along the path which his colleague had first marked out. James believed in the possibility of founding religious faith upon a generalized religious experience that goes beyond special theological interpretations. Royce was more interested in the metaphysical implications of classical Christian ideas. While Royce was equally concerned for the power exercised by religious beliefs in the shaping of daily life, he was more interested than James in the *interpretative* power of ideas. Religion, to Royce, was not a wholly practical affair; the redemption of life includes understanding as well as moral action.

Royce dared to reinterpret classical theological notions through a metaphysical analysis of experience. Like Augustine, he did not shrink from the attempt to give speculative reconstructions of theological doctrines. Royce's combination of metaphysics and theology is possible only where freedom of religious thought exists. In more rigidly controlled religious situations, Protestant and Roman Catholic alike, no such bold interplay between speculative systems and official theological dogma is likely to take place. Unfortunately, recent trends suggest that philosophy and theology have grown increasingly apart. In many quarters theology has become a wholly traditional affair; its methods, language, and content are clearly marked off and they belong to churches and to clergy. Philosophy, on the other hand, exists in another compartment and according to some it is synonymous with skepticism and anti-religion. Royce sought to overcome this kind of mutual separation and suspicion. He tried to force the believer to a deeper understanding of his faith, including a proper respect for the intellectual difficulties, by subjecting ancient ideas to philosophical scrutiny. He sought to show the philosophically minded that there is a logical and experiential content in many classical theological doctrines.

Royce's metaphysical idealism could not maintain itself on the American scene. It was not practical enough and, for all of Royce's own interest in scientific topics, his thought did not seem to others to be sufficiently imbued with the scientific spirit. The fact is that American philosophy was to lose its independence in the following decades, abandoning many of its traditional concerns because of excessive anxiety over its own imprecision in the face of the dazzling successes of the natural sciences. There were many difficulties with Royce's philosophy — it often had an unctuous tone, it did not do justice to the physical world and it did not attract followers endowed with metaphysical interest — but he carried on the grand tradition of interpreting our life and world from a philosophical standpoint. Royce did not accept the view taken over by many later American thinkers that philosophy has been superseded by the natural sciences and that, if it has a life at all, it can be no more than that of methodology or theory of language. He was the most completely systematic American philosopher. Perhaps American life is too varied and plural in its interests to allow for a unified view of things, but we may well ask whether an integral life does not demand more unity than is evident in the piecemeal approach which allows you to deal with problems one at a time without forcing you to become clear about your fundamental and enduring aims. Royce tried to formulate such aims for his own time. We need not accept his results in order to learn from him the need to become aware of our own most basic beliefs.

I V

John Dewey: EXPERIENCE, EXPERIMENT, AND

THE METHOD OF INTELLIGENCE

A growing America, rapidly becoming aware of its power and of the possibility of creating the most advanced technological society in history, faced too many practical problems to rest content with a lofty vision of reality as a whole. Royce's philosophy had its own contribution to make, but his thought did not seem at all fitted to help in the solution of immediate problems. There were cities to be built, social and legal systems to be established, problems of education and human welfare to be solved. America was preparing to exploit untold resources under the earth and to erect on its surface those giants of steel and concrete which were to become the universal symbols of American enterprise and engineering skill. Attention was focused on the here and now; the Absolute Self who surveys all at one glance seemed out of place in the midst of so much practical endeavor.

To many it appeared wisest to forget about the Eternal and the soul of man in order to devote the fullest attention to the temporal and its demands. The situation called for a type of mind more concerned with changing things than with interpreting their superhuman value. It was, in short, time for a new kind of practical philosophy, a philosophy more concerned for social realities than that of James and more involved in solving immediate problems than that of Royce. John Dewey was the man who developed that philosophy and he did so with a vigor which was thoroughly in accord with the tenor of American life.

Dewey was reared in the atmosphere of nineteenth-century rural Vermont; he lived to see his philosophy embodied in the urban metropolis and in the technological society of twentieth-century America. In many ways Dewey was *the* American philosopher of the first half of this century; his thought was a moving force in, and a reflected image of, much that was at the center of American life up to the end of the Second World War. His conception of science as a tool helped to foster its application to the problems of society; science for Dewey did not mean the traditional search for knowledge on its own account, but rather a body of ideas and hypotheses to be used for controlling the environment. His interest in social, political, and economic affairs, and his belief that controlled inquiry would result in the solution of many problems in these areas, had a powerful effect on the development of the social sciences. Dewey contributed to the formation of an optimistic outlook on the world through his conviction that human problems are due mainly to ignorance and superstition, and that they can be solved by the attainment of knowledge. He summed up and was spokesman for America's expanding technological faith. His influence has extended to almost every region of our life from education to the world of art, from ethics to social science.

The surest indication of the power of his thought is in the responses it has called forth. To many his words were gospel, and to them he stood as the champion of science and freedom against the powers of obscurantism and special privilege. To others his philosophy represented only the material side of human life — the body without the soul — and they objected strenuously to his setting aside religion in favor of new values supposedly derived from science. The curious fact is that both sides, the partisans as well as the critics, can find support for their judgments; the major problem at present is to discover to what extent each was right and each wrong.

Dewey was born in 1859, the year Darwin published *The Origin of Species.* The coincidence may serve as a symbol; not since Aristotle has any philosopher built his thought so completely on biological foundations. The vision of man as a changing and developing being in the midst of an environment which fosters and at the same time threatens his life was decisive for Dewey. Organism and environment, development and struggle, precariousness and stability — these are the basic ingredients of the cosmic mixture. We must see how Dewey managed to put them together in the unifying medium of *Experience.* This is his central concept; to understand it and its relations to Nature is to understand the essential meaning of Dewey's philosophy.

Dewey's own intellectual odyssey starts with the sort of idealism we associate with the name of Hegel and it ends with the philosophy of instrumentalism, a naturalistic version of that thoroughgoing criticism of abstractions which Hegel carried through so brilliantly, even if darkly, in the *Phenomenology of Mind.* There is no point in the attempt to keep Dewey's Hegelian background a secret; not only has the secret long been revealed, but much of what is sound in Dewey's thought can be traced to the tradition stemming from Aristotle and Plato which Hegel represented. But, like many others, Dewey felt that the modern idealist tradition, especially in its rationalistic form, failed to do justice to the natural world and to the brute facts of nature. Consequently, he set out to remedy this defect and at the same time to call into question the degradation of practice in the face of theory, which seemed to him characteristic of the intellectualist tradition since the days of the Greeks. His theory of empirical knowledge was aimed at overcoming the divorce between theory and practice; at the heart of instrumentalism was the idea that science is the best living example of the co-operation between doing and knowing. Dewey believed that if science can be shown to be a combination of experimental doing and theoretical construction, the disparagement of practice in the face of theory can no longer be maintained.

There are, however, limits to our success in seeking to understand a philosopher by tracing out his antecedents. However much Dewey himself may have used an historical or genetic method in the posing of his own problems, we must attempt to understand his resolutions of these problems in their own terms. We must see them as his active response to the challenges of the environment and the culture of his time. For the fact is that the more original, focused, and coherent a philosopher's views are, the more they demand that we treat them in themselves. We must take our cue from Dewey's conclusions and leave the matter of discovering their antecedents to others.

To elucidate Dewey's theory of experience is at the same time to set forth his conception of man. Man is, to be sure, always seen as a creature in nature; it is obvious enough that we cannot neglect the environment, but it is equally important that we not lose sight of man himself, who is the wielder of the scientific instrument and the one who has the experience which is to direct its use. Dewey was fond of saying, and he repeated the point often, that while James stressed the psychological make-up of man and Peirce focused on the logical aspects of things, he was determined to view man from a *biological* standpoint. This is not to say that Dewey neglected either psychology or logic — he wrote books on both subjects — but rather that he saw man as fundamentally an organism developing in time, as a creature whose life can best be described in terms of public and objective relations with an environing medium, natural as well as cultural. Private consciousness and the interpretation of things from the standpoint of individual psychology always made Dewey uneasy. The primary source of his dissatisfaction with the empiricism of the British tradition was its reliance upon sensation and the private mind in which sensations must reside. Dewey's philosophy from beginning to end is opposed to a sensationalist psychology; his own reconstruction of the notion of experience had as its aim the elimination of the classical view according to which the immediate data of sense, directly apprehended by the individual mind, constitute the subject matter of knowledge. For Dewey, sensation is never immediate; insofar as it can be found at all, it is not certain and, above all, when it is taken all by itself, it is not knowledge. To grasp this point is to be at the center of Dewey's conception of experience. And to understand experience is to understand man since man is the being of experience *par excellence*.

In a paper, "The Reflex Arc Concept in Psychology," written just before the turn of the century, Dewey turned his attention to what was known as the "reflex arc" concept in the psychological theory of the time. The basic point made in that paper reveals the fundamental tendency in Dewey's philosophy: translate the static into the dynamic and replace substances or entities with functions. While acknowledging the superiority of the reflex arc concept over previous explanations, he attacked it nevertheless for preserving ancient and dubious distinctions. Dewey objected particularly to the analysis of experience-situations into distinct entities such as "sensation," "ideas," "actions," and so forth. Instead he made a plea for taking experience as an organic process that has different aspects within it, and differences of function, but lacks distinct entities. The stimulus-response analysis appeared to him the same as saying that experience is a matter of "sensations" which fall on us from the blue and then produce, in some wholly mechanical way, an activity called the "motor response." His point can be seen clearly if we take his own example: the child, seeing a burning candle, at once reaches out to grasp it, burns its hand, and then immediately withdraws it in a seemingly involuntary way. For Dewey the initial state is not that of "sensation" — seeing the light as a disconnected sensory datum — but rather that of *looking*, which is itself an act and one which involves motion of the body, fixing of the head, eyes, and so forth. The looking, which is the primary act, does stimulate another act, namely the grasping, but Dewey takes this as a "co-ordination" of sensori-motor elements and not as the stimulus from a bare sensation. The activity of looking carries with it the grasping as a continuation of the process; the consequent pain-heat quality goes along with muscular and ocular sensations. The situation contains a *circle* of activity rather than an arc and, in the future, when the child is in a similar situation, the initial activity of looking carries with it the rest of the resulting cycle. What we have is a development of experience rather than the substitution of one fixed element for another.

It seems safe to conclude, although Dewey was never as clear as he might have been on this matter, that sensation is not ruled out in every sense of the term. It is rather that there is no such thing as a "bare" sensation which breaks in upon us without having its context furnished by the environment and the ongoing life of the person whose experience the sensation is. The "looking-grasping-withdrawing" sequence represents a continuous organic process; it signals the enrichment of experience through growth rather than a substitution of distinct psychic existences for one another. There is no "pure" sensation at the outset because the child is *looking* and not merely *seeing;* there is no "pure" motor reaction at the end, because the child's action is a *response to* conditions which set the cycle going in the first place. The sequence ceases to be a set of disconnected events as soon as we discern the purposive pattern in it. Dewey's point is that it is only when we *first* consider the series of occurrences as directed toward an end, that we make the attempt to distinguish the stimulus from the response.

Dewey's paper on the reflex arc is instructive not only because of the introduction it gives us to his general philosophical practice — the enclosing of previous distinctions and divisions within a wider organic unity, where they become functions or stages of a process rather than distinct existences — but because it foreshadows his conception of experience. The analysis presented is too limited in scope to support all that Dewey ultimately wants to claim — the conclusion, in fact, goes considerably beyond what can be supported by the body of the paper — but it represents the earliest formulation of his theory of experience. The initial stage of a process of experience, the "stimulus" in the older psychology, is taken to mean the encounter of conditions which must be met in some way; the consequent action or reaction, the "response" in the older theory, represents the way in which the conditions are to be met. We do not have here as yet the explicit identification of the stimulus with the problematic situation, nor of the response with the resolution and reconstitution of the disturbed state of affairs, but we surely have the seeds of such a view. It is clear that the later instrumentalist theory of experience which stresses its organic character, its capacity for growth, and its purposeful orientation, is no more than a development of the basic criticisms set forth in this early paper.

Dewey described man as an organism, and it is clear that he chose this term because he wanted to emphasize the facts of growth and change as brought together in the unity of a living whole. At the same time he aimed at avoiding the various idealistic identifications of man with an ego, soul, mind, or transcendental subject, though he admitted with characteristic candor late in life that he never developed an adequate theory of personality. But apart from such considerations, the idea of organism was well adapted to his needs. It pointed both to a structured being fitted to perform specific functions and to a living whole capable of responding to the surrounding medium of its life. To speak of an organism was to focus attention upon a unified being easily locatable in the world and not upon a private consciousness difficult to find and approach. The Darwinian picture of things was always in the back of Dewey's mind and every important concept in his philosophy — inquiry, intelligence, experience, science — becomes intelligible only against the polarity of organism and environment and the interactions between them.

Dewey had no objections to the classical definition of man as the rational animal and, to a greater degree than has been recognized, he regarded himself as carrying on the Greek tradition and the ideal of human rationality. But, like James, he did not think of reason as a fixed possession or substance delivered full blown to each man at birth; he thought of reason as a *power* and of rationality as an ideal to be achieved in the course of a struggle with the outer world. Taking his cue from the Darwinian hypothesis, he saw powers and functions where others saw substances, and he sought the key to everything in the checkered story of its development through time and the vicissitudes of historical process. Man has the power to be intelligent and he has the power of intelligence, but both must be seen as emerging from a more ultimate organic process. Reason, its exercise in thinking and its successful completion in knowledge, all have biological and cultural foundations; like the other pragmatists, Dewey sought to uncover the antecedents of thought and to lay hold of the specific conditions in accordance with which it comes into play. Man is not a theoretical animal who is always aiming at the complete and disinterested knowledge of things; he is primarily an organism who must struggle against, and at the same time co-operate with, the environment in order to survive. The asking of questions, that first indication of intelligent life, is prompted by conditions and situations in the total environment; it is not a self-contained activity. The power of intelligence is first revealed in situations which lead to questions, and its perfection consists in the successful meeting of the challenge. The belief that thinking takes place under, and is at least partially determined by, conditions not entirely set by thinking itself is one of the major beliefs of pragmatism. Dewey went further than all others in developing this belief.

Man does not have intelligence as a fixed possession; according to the theory, intelligence is an achievement, and there are conditions surrounding its development and the time when it is called into play. How does thinking arise and what are its conditions? Dewey devoted a great deal of time to this question and we would be justified in interpreting a large part of his thought as the systematic attempt to answer it. The context of thought was of constant concern to him; the reason for that concern is not hard to find. When we know the conditions under which reflective thought arises we have a clue to the *function* of thought. We come here to the heart of Dewey's position: thought is not self-contained but has a function to perform in relation to the environment, and that function is the clue to its nature. Its function is set by the circumstances under which it comes into being; it appears when life-situations press in upon us, tax our old ideas and habitual actions, and confront us with problems which, on the basis of present resources, we are unable to resolve. Dewey distinguished between bare consciousness as a constant accompaniment of our waking life, and *reflective* thought which is called into being only when we face difficulties and find that habitual responses no longer work or deal effectively with the matter at hand. Reflective thought is thought acutely aware of the situation; it seeks to grasp what we are about, and why we are unable to proceed in the normal or regular manner. It seeks for clues as to the nature of the obstacle before us and the way in which it might be removed. Reflective thought is an active response to the challenge of the environment; when it is called into play, its nature is revealed and with it the nature of a rational being.

The rise of reflective thought represents a late and very highly developed response to the environment in which man finds himself. Human history records earlier and different responses on the part of man to the basic character of existence. The question arising is this: What is there about the world and the life of man in it which calls for a reflective response upon our part? The answer is given in the fact that the world of empirical things includes the uncertain, the unpredictable, and the hazardous; the world is, in short, a precarious place in which to live and nothing in it has its survival guaranteed in advance. Starting with this uncertain world, Dewey was able to interpret man's characteristic responses to his environment — propitiation of the gods, magic, ritual practices, art, and, most recently, scientific intelligence — as essentially responses of *control*, in which the aim is to minimize the precarious and build the more stable. The most basic trait of existence — its uncertain, doubtful, and hazardous character — provides at the same time the chief clue to man's distinctive nature. Man is the being who can grasp and confront the precarious and doubtful *as such;* he is capable of grasping the generic character of existence and, in finding that this character means a problem, he can respond to the challenge with his own appropriate weapons. But while the nature of man and his resources for shaping his destiny occupied the center of Dewey's attention, we must not overlook the importance of the surrounding environment which is our natural habitat.

Following the lead of Hegel, and indeed of all dialectical philosophers who have acknowledged the important role played by contraries, opposites, and polarities in reality, Dewey laid stress upon the mutual involvement of the precarious and the stable in all existence. Discord between the two generates problems and gives to life its poignancy, adventure, and possibility for growth; harmony between the two defines our satisfactions and points to the fulfillments which, as we say, make life worthwhile. "A purely stable world," writes Dewey, "permits no illusions, but neither is it clothed with ideals." That total adjustment of every part to every other, which is the hallmark of a continuous and uninterrupted process, represents a state very different from the one in which man actually lives. Pure nature exclusive of man does not have this character; if we put man in the picture, the situation is even further removed from the model of the fully adjusted process. For man is a being of complex needs and he is capable of envisaging the difference between the better and the worse; these very facts point to a discord or lack of total adjustment between his own being and the world surrounding him. Dewey was, to be sure, not completely of one mind regarding the relation of man to nature. At times he sought to

derive mind and intelligence from the fact of discord in things
and from the fact that man envisages the problematic nature
of himself and his world; at others, he saw that, while you may
try to *define* man as the being who can respond to "the doubtful as such," you still need to presuppose a being who already
has the capacity of grasping the doubtful as such. Mind and
intelligence have the peculiar character that if you try to define them in terms of some actual operation which is or can be
performed, you will always find that the operation in question
turns out to be the sort of thing which only a being with mind
or intelligence can perform. There are, in fact, many beings
in nature whose actual situation is "problematic" (this is all
the more so in Dewey's terms, since he repeatedly argued that
the "problematic" character of things is "in the situation" and
not merely in the mind of any being) but, as far as we are able
to say, they are unable to apprehend their "problem" or respond to it *as such*. The reason is not that their situation is not
really problematic, but rather that the very meaning of a problematic situation is, in part at least, a function of a being who
is already aware and able to grasp the total character of a
situation, compare it with other situations, envisage alternatives, and so forth. This means that while the meaning of mind
and intelligence is surely bound up with the precarious character of the environment, the facts of discord and maladjust-
ment, that meaning cannot be identical with response to such
a challenge because the power to become aware of the predicament itself is possible only for a being endowed with
mind. There are several topics here for further consideration;
for the present, we must return to the conception of man,
which is at the heart of the instrumentalist theory.

Dewey was fond of saying that whereas the British empirical tradition invariably defined man in psychological terms,
and the idealist tradition in terms of mind and reason, his view

aimed at conceiving man in *biological* terms. No man will grasp Dewey's thought who does not take the statement both seriously and literally. It does not mean that Dewey thought of man solely in physiological terms; his position is far more subtle. It does mean that man is not to be understood·primarily as a theoretical knower who merely represents the world through "ideas" in the mind. For Dewey, we do not start within the mind and we do not start with the elements of certainty — simple ideas of sense or clear and distinct ideas of reason. We start instead with man as a complex organism set within an environment of change, flux, precariousness, and stability. The biological orientation means setting out from the organism-environment polarity and then showing how all of the distinctions of complex and mature experience emerge from that primordial situation. Instead of starting with abstract, precise, and therefore "reflected products," we are to begin with the more vague and confused mass of things, meanings, tendencies, drives, interests, and feelings which arise out of the interaction between a living organism and an evolving environment. Dewey, like James, did not regard experience as clear-cut sensible content from the start, but saw it rather as a "booming, buzzing confusion" which we attack by means of creative intelligence with the aim of reducing it to order and to knowledge. In referring to this general outlook as a biological approach, Dewey was emphasizing the organic character of man and the continuous character of the environment. Above all, he tried to avoid any starting point "inside" the mind; man is primarily an organism and, while reflective thought turns out to be the most important function of that organism, we must not conceive of human nature exclusively in cognitive terms. Life encompasses more than thought alone. To begin the account of things by starting within the mind means not only placing undue emphasis upon the psychological dimension, but it involves us as well in throwing a blanket of mind, so to speak, over a total situation that cannot be reduced to the status of an object of knowledge.

That Dewey's man is a man of technological skill and resources, there can be no doubt; instrumentalism is the philosophical expression of practical reason aimed at transforming the face of nature and at civilizing human nature in the process. Dewey's man is a man of *control*. Bacon had said that knowledge is power; instrumentalism means taking that statement seriously. It means believing in human intelligence as the best instrument for mastering the instability of existence and for enhancing the value of human life. Control, since it represents an ultimate goal and is possible only through fully developed intelligence, appears very late in the unfolding of the human drama. Human nature manifests itself in a succession of stages, which may be viewed both as steps in a temporal development and as permanent structural features of the self. Human development starts with impulse and what are generally called natural instincts, it passes into habits and their embodiment in custom, and finally issues in intelligence where we become clearly aware of the *meaning* of the preceding stages and of the fuller proportions of the situation in which we exist. Means and ends exist prior to the development of intelligence, but only for intelligent beings can they be said to come "into view."

The light thrown upon Dewey's theory of man by the account of this development is considerable. Impulse, though in a sense the most primitive and elemental feature of the human species, cannot be considered first because, for Dewey, original, unlearned activity is meaningless until it is interpreted in a social situation. While they are more primitive than habits which are learned responses, native activities take on their meaning in relation to the behavior of others. Dewey's point is that anger, for example, is no more than a blind outburst or spasm on the part of the individual organism until it is directed by the presence of *other* persons. A man, it would appear, cannot be angry at himself or, if Dewey would admit that he can, it is only because the individual is already a social being in himself. Dewey claimed that for a human being, a being with language and the capacity to remember and anticipate, there can be no purely original or "natural" traits which we can isolate and understand apart from the cultural and social situation. While he was not unaware of man's endowment with powers and abilities stemming from the biological species to which he belongs, Dewey realized that we have no access to such an endowment except as it expresses itself in concrete life, which means in the social and cultural context. What Dewey did not see is that the individual has an inner life of his own which is itself *social* in character just because it is an endless dialogue of the self with itself. It is not that this inner life can take the place of common intercourse with other selves, but that it is not necessary, in order to escape a doctrine of blind, original instincts, to reduce meaning to its public context. There is private social intercourse as well, and the individual can learn something from his own confrontation with himself no less than from his encounter with others. Dewey repeatedly underestimated this.

Failure, however, to do full justice to man's inner life does not alter the fact that Dewey was a master in the analysis of man's outer or public life. His doctrine of habit plays a central role in that analysis. Ongoing life is habitual life, life propelled forward less by conscious plans and programs than by learned patterns and responses. Habits are basically predispositions which develop in response to the demand for activities of a certain kind; they are, as Dewey repeatedly emphasized, more intimately ourselves than are conscious choices and resolutions to follow general principles. A misconception often encountered in discussions of Dewey takes the form of saying that habit and intelligent control are mutually exclusive. It would be more accurate to say that habits represent institutionalized conceptions in which, to borrow the vivid language of Peirce, ideas become fixed in our muscles. Reflective thought or intelligence is brought into play when habitual action breaks down or becomes inadequate, but there is no need to oppose the two since it is one of the aims of reflective thought to lead to new habits or patterns of action. And this can be done only if the matter is approached in a fresh way and without the traditional separation of means from ends. This was one of Dewey's favorite topics and it played a large part in his philosophy.

In analyzing the idea of a *course* of action — an end result with a well-ordered series of acts serving as means — Dewey maintained that "means and ends are two names for the same reality." This conclusion is thoroughly dependent upon his other claim that the distinction represents not a division in reality so much as a distinction in judgment. His seemingly paradoxical view can be simply expressed. To envisage an end or goal is at the same time to envisage some course of action leading up to it; an end is the last member of a chain of means. In order to accomplish the result the *first* consideration is to find the first member in the series of means; we must get started or set the course of action in motion. Finding this first means is our first end. The means closest to us are our own habits; in starting with them we are starting with something actual, something already there. We are not imposing "ideas" from outside which are without a basis in the physiological or mental constitution of the person. Instead we are starting with tendencies already established and by directing them through the chain of further acts we are able to arrive at that last result which is the end. The whole process is continuous in the sense that to think of the end without the means is to think a disconnected event which has, as we say, "no means" of getting itself realized. On the other hand, a course of action has its unity as a genuine sequence, instead of a random series, in virtue of the fact that the separate acts which go to make it up are means chosen and performed because they lead to that last event which is the end.

The control and reshaping of habits lead naturally to the question as to the mutability of human nature; can the leopard change his spots? What is human nature and what sort of control, if any, is possible? This question lies at the root of an instrumental philosophy. For if intelligence is to be an instrument we shall want to know whether it has any power to transform the being who wields it. The question is not confined to the transforming power of intelligence, however. It concerns the entire human constitution and serves at the same time to focus attention upon the distinction between nature and culture. As in most of his solutions, Dewey here adopts a mediating position, a synthesis of original impulse and acquired habit. On the one hand, man inherits a certain constitution as a member of the biological order and it will not do to suppose that schemes of reason's devising, no matter how admirable in both form and intent, can simply be imposed from outside. Instinct and original impulse, on the other hand, do not represent a fixed inheritance that is beyond the reach of man's ability to control, modify, and redirect. Contrary to a well-received view, Dewey argued that the evils in human existence, which we generally attribute to an unalterable human nature, must be understood as stemming not from instincts but from the "inertness of established habit." Man is a creature neither of impulse nor of reason — the favorite raw materials, respectively, of materialists and idealists — but of *habit*, which is the meeting point of the two and the stuff from which both man and culture are made. The singling out of habit as the essential feature of man is of the utmost importance to Dewey's entire outlook. For if man is primarily a creature of habit and habits are accessible to human intelligence, many of the most pervasive ills of human history *can* be attacked, and they *should* be, in principle at least, subject to elimination.

The attack upon war, for example, as the one evil that in every age threatens human life with destruction, is launched through the gigantic effort to modify established habits. This does not happen merely by confronting organic patterns existing in individuals and reinforced by institutions and custom with ideas or ideal goals. Dewey's position is more subtle. Habits or learned responses arise under specific conditions; to modify them we must effect changes in the existing conditions. This does not happen merely by changing our ideas — the changing of habits requires the effective power of original impulse. The direction of the latter is determined by acquired habits, but these in turn can be modified only by the redirection of impulse. Dewey was well aware that catastrophes and large-scale social upheavals often succeed in breaking this vicious circle, but he hoped for a less extreme solution. His proposal at this point goes to the heart of his own social idealism and indeed to that of the American nation. The one direction in which hope can be found is in the direction of youth and their training. *Education* is the key.

The idea of universal education — taken more seriously in America than in any other part of the world during the past century — has frequently been understood only in terms of the democracy of opportunity. That it is intimately connected with the ideal of extending to every man an equal opportunity to develop his own potentialities and talents is of course true. But there is a more subtle reason behind the idea of *universal* education in Dewey's thinking; it means the education of an *entire* people, the education of a nation and, through them, the education of an age. It means the redirection of impulse and the modification of habit all across the culture at large. This is something very different from the education, in an established tradition, of a few whose task it will then be to guide and direct the others. It is rather the enterprise of redirecting the entire culture at a most elemental level. Social transformation — the changing of basic social, economic, and political conditions — has a better chance of success if the total population is involved.

If we recall the vicious circle of impulse and habit, the purpose behind the demand for universal education is clarified. Instead of our having to look for catastrophic upheaval to change the situation determining the dominant habits of the culture, we entertain the hope that some more civilized avenue may be open to us. Dewey found that avenue in education, but education of the sort that is available to every man in every walk of life. Unless it is to extend itself over the entire culture and penetrate to its foundation, education proves ineffective as a solution to the problem of the vicious circle. The extent of education, the demand that it be no less than universal, is finally bound up with the need to find a way of reorienting society at large. Dewey's own statement is at once instructive and inspiring; in *Human Nature and Conduct* (1922) he wrote:

> The idea of universal education is as yet hardly a century old, and it is still much more of an idea than a fact . . . Hence it is easy to point out defects and perversions in every existing school system. It is easy for a critic to ridicule the religious devotion to education which has characterized for example the American republic. It is easy to represent it as zeal without knowledge, fanatical faith without understanding. And yet

the cold fact of the situation is that the chief means of continuous, graded, economical improvement and social rectification lies in utilizing the opportunities of educating the young to modify prevailing types of thought and desire.*

The candor, the concern for fact, and the unwillingness to abandon an ideal merely because it is difficult to realize are traits which we must associate at once with the mind of Dewey (and, for that matter, with the general spirit of philosophical thinking in America).

Dewey's theory of experience embraces not only man and his nature, but it leads on ultimately to a consideration of intelligence and to science. For Dewey science is the most highly developed form of human intelligence and it is man's chief weapon in the struggle for existence. Instrumentalism means the doctrine that mind or intelligence exists as a problem-solving power and that this function is more important than pursuing the ideal of a purely theoretical and comprehensive knowledge of all things. It is more than a philosophy of technological society, although it is that too; instrumentalism is the attempt to show how the practical application of science in technology represents a way of understanding the synthesis of theory and practice, of contemplation and action. Even more, by taking seriously the role of experiment, of practical manipulation, in the actual attainment of knowledge, Dewey aimed at breaking down the perennial opposition between technical skill — knowing how — and theoretical knowledge — knowing that and knowing why. The latter point marks the most subtle contribution of his form of pragmatism. It amounts to much more than saying that ideas have or should have practical consequences; it aims at showing how practice itself is woven into the fabric of science. The secrets of nature and the

* Modern Library Edition, p. 127.

principles governing the inner working of things are not to be gained merely by looking or even by reasoning; these secrets yield to our persistent inquiry only insofar as we ourselves intervene and try out various alternatives. The behavior of all things under the earth and beyond the stars can be discovered only through controlling events, trying out different possibilities — practicing, one might say — in order to see how things actually work. Science, in short, means experiment and experiment is action and practice. Dewey's contention was that if the very prosecution of scientific inquiry requires action and manipulation on our part, there cannot be an ultimate opposition between knowing and doing.

There are many signs that Dewey's interpretation of science has not been understood and there are indications that the culture at large has not yet succeeded in grasping the full meaning of science's impact upon modern life. Instrumentalism means that intelligence is a tool or weapon to be used for human purposes, and insofar as science is regarded as the most perfect form of intelligence it takes on the status of the instrument par excellence. But this straightforward explanation, true though it certainly is, may lead us to omit a more subtle and important point. Science, for Dewey, meant a living illustration of the intimate connection which can and must exist between knowing and doing. This is the deeper truth. In stressing the point that science is not the passive reception of facts or registry of them, existing complete and finished, Dewey was trying to emphasize the active intervention which the knower must make. Experiment is the key. To gain knowledge we must act, devise instruments and situations whereby things can be induced to reveal their characteristic behavior. When Darwin said, thinking of the Book of Job, that we must *speak to* the earth in order to learn, he was calling attention to one important aspect of the situation: to discover answers, one must put questions. Our success in discovering the secrets of nature will depend upon our ingenuity in interrogation. Dewey went further. Speak to the earth we must, but in order to obtain and understand the answers, it is necessary to *anticipate* nature by devising special experimental situations in which we can observe the effects of things upon each other at will. We are not, as Kant saw, in nature's leading strings; we can manipulate things and bring them into the laboratory. We can, in short, bring them out of their "natural" habitat in order to observe their behavior under conditions in accordance with our own hypotheses.

The particular role played by experiment in the development of modern science had for Dewey the special philosophical significance that action, practice, and behavior cannot be alien to thought, and that the ancient tendency to disparage practice in favor of theory and contemplative thought is mistaken. Dewey took it that the actual fact of science furnishes us with a living example of the essential connection existing between thought and action. Hence if we think of instrumentalism merely as the doctrine that scientific knowledge, *once achieved,* can be used or applied for practical purposes in engineering and technology, we shall have understood but a part of the truth. The rest of the story becomes clear only when we see that the achievement of knowledge itself is a process in which human activity plays a vital role. Between the initial situation in which a problem presents itself and the point at which a resolution is reached, there intervenes an experimental stage. In this interval we are engaged not merely in the passive recording of more facts, but in the active devising of experimental situations in which we literally force reality to answer our questions. The results, expressed as theoretical conclusions, represent the last stage of a process which is more than a development of thought; it stands as the outcome of *activities* guided by ideas and is thus the effective product of both practical endeavor and intellectual insight. Science for Dewey was more than technology, despite the fact that he taught us to think of it in technological terms. Science was for him the best and most vivid example of the marriage of theory and action; it seemed to him that the two cannot really be alien to each other if their co-operation can produce such success.

It is thus an oversimplification (and one which has far-reaching consequences) to suppose that the "practical" and "pragmatic" conception of science held by one of the most distinguished philosophers on the American scene means the reduction of science to its instrumental value. A deeper understanding makes it plain that the action and practice which Dewey emphasized so much are not confined merely to the application of knowledge, but to the difficult business of acquiring it in the first place. The fact that the secrets of nature cannot be disclosed without *experiment*, practical manipulation, and active intervention on the part of man, helps us to understand that thought and action are *essentially* connected with each other. Unfortunately, this more subtle point has rarely been understood; most have been content to interpret the American understanding of science as wholly technological, failing at the same time to grasp the significance of Dewey's idea. With his conception of science as a thoroughly experimental affair, Dewey intended to advance the solution to the ancient problem of theory and practice. Instead of a mere exaltation of practice in the face of the sort of profound theory usually associated with European traditions of thought, Dewey's interpretation actually means a more penetrating theory in which theory itself becomes integrated with practical activity. Perhaps the widespread failure to grasp the novelty of the idea is to be attributed to the standard prejudice with which many outside of America tend to view our ideas. They look only to the practice itself, instead of seeing that the real point is to be found in a new *conception of practice,* aimed at revealing its importance in a total scheme of things. There can be no doubt that Dewey had a high regard for practical activity, but he was even more interested in *understanding* the meaning of practical activity in human affairs. We shall miss an important part of what he had to say if we suppose that his concern for practical theories diverted him from trying to develop a coherent *theory* of practice.

The importance of practice is further emphasized by a problem that engaged Dewey from the beginning to the end of his career: How to bridge the gulf between science and value? It was one of the major tasks of instrumentalism to solve this question. In his later years particularly, he returned to the matter of showing how the method of intelligence must be used in treating those questions regarded as having to do with "value," and he was resolutely opposed to any suggestion that this method is confined to the knowledge of nature alone. One of the most controversial doctrines of his philosophy was the claim that somehow all of our values are rooted in science and that anyone who proposes to ignore science in the discovery of values can be nothing but a moral dogmatist.

Dewey was suspicious of any view which would confine value to a narrow sphere of "moral" rules. The problem, in fact, of properly delimiting the moral aspect of life was never solved by him, and there remains a tension in his thought between value as it figures in *any* situation involving alternative courses of action and those situations which have a definite moral bearing in virtue of their peculiar connection with human character and integrity. Value and evaluation for Dewey enter wherever alternative ways of behavior arise; alternatives mean choice and choice involves us at once in distinguishing the better from the worse way of proceeding. Dewey hoped, by the projection of worthy goals rooted in nature and human nature, to show that the whole problem of value consists in discovering the best means and materials for realizing the goals we prize. We are not to suppose that his view is one more variation on the ancient thesis that whereas means are to be determined through empirical knowledge, ends are pure products of desire or fancy. On the contrary, Dewey's doctrine of the intimate connection between ends and means was designed to overcome the opposition between the two and to show that ends themselves are somehow subject to determination through the same method of intelligence required for deciding on means and materials. The entire theory is more subtle than at first appears and the best way of elucidating its major features is to show how Dewey developed it in opposition to both the psychological utilitarianism which held sway in the British tradition of ethics and the rationalism often associated with the German ethical tradition originating with Kant.

Like Aristotle, Dewey was willing to *begin* his reflection on values with the concrete experiences of desire and satisfaction. Unlike the proponents of modern theories of value based on desire, however, he was not willing to let reflection *end* there. The fact that something is desired or some state of affairs is enjoyed can be taken into account and put down among the so-called data of ethics. But taken all by themselves, these facts are not the solution to the problem of value; they are at best materials with which to formulate that problem. We do not rest with the bare fact that something is desired or found satisfying; such a fact is no more than an autobiographical report, and even if we could multiply the fact many times over by counting heads and asking people what they do in fact desire, we would not yet have reached a genuine value. As Dewey puts it, "To say that something is enjoyed is to make a statement about a fact . . . it is not to judge the value of that fact." He saw, as many proponents of so-called empirical theories of value have not, that only some of our desires represent defensible values and that, while it may always accompany the value situation, desire is an insufficient basis on which to settle the question of the genuinely valuable. Dewey's response is characteristic; instead of arguing, after the fashion of some rationalists, that the insufficiency of desire as a criterion means that we must appeal to universal rational insights, he urged us to look into the conditions of desire and the natures of the objects desired. At this turning point, the heart of his position is revealed. It is not bare desire or approval which forms the foundation of value and evaluation, but *desire informed by criticism.* What is desired *after* we have investigated the natures of things and the mechanics of our own desiring will come closer to what ought to be desired or what would be good to desire. Casual liking or desiring has no inherent value; the question is, What is needed if we are to make a transition from casual to critical liking? Between the initial desires and enjoyments, which give rise to reflection in the moral situation, and the discovery of desires approved on reflection, falls the method of intelligence. The underlying pattern of Dewey's thought is continued and reinforced; between a problem and its resolution we must always interject a rational method. In the moral situation this means that between casual desire and values approved on reflection there must come a process of knowledge and critical inquiry. Science — in this case, knowledge of the potentialities and powers of things together with basic insight into the nature of man and his needs — instead of being alien to ethics, turns out to be indispensable.

Everything depends on the shift of attention away from the

individual self and its inner psychology. Rather than centering on the feelings of the one who judges or decides, attention is drawn to the conditions in accordance with which things happen and to the capacities of things for satisfying human needs. The discovery that an object is satisfying means no more than the fact that this object has actually satisfied someone; we have here a report about what William James would have called "finished fact," and it belongs to the past. Dewey is interested in something more than the report of accomplished fact; he demands to know what is involved in the further act of appraisal or evaluation. A genuine value means that something is *satisfactory* — not merely satisfying — and this in turn means that whatever we judge to be good or valuable is *capable* of fulfilling certain conditions when called upon to do so. We are interested, in short, in the way things *would* or should behave under certain circumstances and in their capacities to be "good for" something. To the thirsty man, salt water may harbor an initial enjoyment — the coolness of the liquid in contrast to the burning sensation of thirst — but in the end it forms no genuine value in the situation since reflection tells us at once that salt water cannot fulfill the demand placed upon it. To be *satisfactory* for the thirsty man, to be a genuine good, the salt water would have to be quite other than it is and to be capable of producing effects which, by its own nature, it cannot produce. On reflection, the thirsty man knows that the salt water, despite any initial enjoyment it may give, is actually an evil because it leads to an unsatisfactory situation in the end. Our immediate desires and our natural tendency to satisfy them conspire to produce nothing more than a feeling. Between immediate desire and our tendency to satisfy it in the simplest and most obvious way, reflection and knowledge must intervene. Intelligence steps in to thwart the immediate response. To discover a genuine value or to determine what would really be satisfactory in the situation, requires that we attend to the natures of things and the conditions of their behavior, to what is needed and what will fulfill that need.

The result is that value judgments and reports of appraisal become statements not about actual enjoyments or feelings but about the potentialities and capacities of things; they point out what something may be expected to do and the demands it may be expected to fulfill. At times Dewey described value judgments as hypotheses predicting what should happen under certain circumstances. This interpretation gains in strength if we bear in mind Dewey's instrumental and operational account of science. According to that view, scientific knowledge is construed not as insight into the inner nature or essence of things but rather as controlled anticipation of the connections between things and of the way they may be expected to behave in their many interactions with other things. Value judgments share the character of hypotheses; they state in effect that objects, states of affairs, situations for which value is claimed will prove to be satisfactory for some need, interest, or desire under appropriate conditions. Value and evaluation, in short, are to involve us in the same appeal to consequences or observed behavior which we have learned to expect in all uses of the method of intelligence.

Science and valuation come closer together as a result of mutual reinterpretation. On the one hand, value is no longer to be confined to personal morality and private virtue but must be expanded to include health, flourishing business, education, peace — the things, in short, prized by a vigorous and growing democratic culture — each of which exists under known circumstances and conditions. On the other hand, science must be understood as primarily a method for studying things through manipulation and as tested knowledge concerning the behavior of things and the outcomes of situations. By connecting value with the meeting of conditions and science with the discovery of conditions, Dewey hoped to show that science is indispensable for the process of evaluation.

There can be no doubt that Dewey's way of viewing the matter has some advantages, especially the obvious curb on egoism and subjectivism which it entails. But there are also strong objections to which Dewey, on the whole, paid insufficient attention. He did not solve the problem of how to determine ultimate ends, nor did he take seriously enough the need for a hierarchy of values to provide us with some guidance in situations of conflict. In his passion to show that a practical or realistic idealism will try to bring ideals to bear on existence by paying attention to means and methods, he gradually displaced concern for ends themselves. We are not forced to deny the truth in his often repeated criticism of "mere" idealists who actually weaken their cause by ignoring practical means and consequences, if we enter the objection that Dewey undervalued other and more important sources of value — especially religion. He seemed to think that somehow (one must say "somehow" because it is not clear exactly how) science is able to furnish all the standards of value and evaluation. In response to his own question — "Where will regulation come from if we surrender familiar and traditionally prized values as our directive standards?" — Dewey answered, "Very largely from the findings of the natural sciences." In a vein characteristic of those who hold his position, Dewey hastened to point out that our present knowledge is inadequate to the complexity of the task; since there is no gap in principle between science and value, we may expect to make progress in the right direction simply by the increase of knowledge.

Here we have an outstanding example of America's robust faith in the future and in the saving powers of expanding knowledge and its application to concrete problems. In accordance with this optimistic creed, the human predicament does not center on "conversion" or changing the "eye of the soul" — all such conceptions are subjective, self-centered, and backward looking. Man's problem follows from his inability to apply his knowledge, from his resistance to the idea that science furnishes him with the means of making objective evaluations and not merely with details about the seas and the stars. The hindrances to human progress are largely in the public world, the surrounding environment, not within ourselves; we must look rather in the external world if we are to modify the shape of things, remove obstacles to growth, and liberate the forces of progress. Dewey held this creed, to be sure, in a subtle and well thought out form, but he held it nevertheless. It represents the fundamental faith of America in the first half of the twentieth century.

Dewey was never quite satisfied that he had succeeded in bridging the gap between science and value. In later years he returned to the task and made a final statement of his position in *The Theory of Valuation*. Part of the difficulty stems from the fact that his thesis had never been completely clear. It remained a puzzle in the minds of many as to exactly how the findings of the natural sciences can themselves provide us with the true successors to traditional values. How, in short, does the knowledge which is science bring us into the presence of ends and ideal norms? If, in the traditional pattern, the "fear of the Lord" was the beginning of wisdom and a necessary prelude to that knowledge which must guide and determine life, what can science furnish which will take its place? How shall the fruit of the laboratory replace the philosopher's vision or the prophet's insight in making clear to us what ideals we should strive for and what virtues we should seek to possess? That Dewey believed science could perform these tasks is not in doubt; what remains unclear is exactly how it was to be done.

Value, for Dewey, is an affair of action and of conduct; the notion becomes relevant only when there arise alternative ways of behavior on the part of man or different means and pathways through which a goal is to be reached. Alternatives mean choice; allegiance to the method of intelligence demands that a choice be made on *critical* grounds. Critical choice, in short, involves us in distinguishing between the better and the worse, the good and the bad alternative. Many thinkers in the past began their reflections on the good and on how to make the right choice in this way; thus far there is nothing especially new or startling in Dewey's analysis. Normally, however, it would be thought that the only way in which scientific knowledge might help us in a problematic situation is by informing us as to the "best" (or better) way of achieving some goal previously agreed upon either as desirable or good in itself. The normal supposition would be that science can help us with regard to *means* but that it is unable to furnish us with the materials for determining what ends are valuable. Dewey dissented. Science is not confined to the determination of means alone; it has within itself resources for determining ends. The manner in which this is to be accomplished is through the regulation of our desires. By distinguishing between behavior which is direct and habitual, requiring neither evaluation nor the presence of explicit desire, and behavior which is indirect in the sense that it can take place only after reflection and judgment, Dewey tried to show that the method of intelligence is unavoidable in the framing of ends. When the course of life and events goes along "naturally" and there is no problem or struggle, there is also no need to speak of desires. Desires come into being along with difficulties. Desire for Dewey meant a specific *end in view* and one which is the *proper* end because it represents the solution to a problem. When the situation becomes discordant and a deficiency or lack is felt, habitual action will not suffice. Our sense that something is wrong leads to analysis of the situation; we want to locate the difficulty and resolve it. Genuine desire, as distinct from wish, whim, fancy, and day-dreaming, exists when there is the clear intention, expressed as an end in view, to overcome the obstacle and set the situation right again. Since ends, Dewey argued, are no more than the last stage in a series of events which serve as means, they are organically connected with the factors and conditions which lead up to them. The same is true of a desire as an end in view. It can be a genuine desire only insofar as it results from the attempt to grasp the situation and locate the difficulty in order to determine what actual means or series of events will lead to a resolution. Whims and fancies are ruled out as desires and ends in view precisely because they remain unconnected with acts and materials which would realize them. Scientific knowledge becomes relevant to the determination of ends just because it alone can inform us regarding the natures of things and the courses of action which will lead to specified results. This information, in turn, is necessary for the framing of desires or ends in view that can resolve problematic situations.

There are at least two questions to be raised. The first concerns the truth of the claim that means — the better, most-to-be-valued means — can always be best determined by following the lead of theoretical knowledge. The second asks exactly how knowledge of the conditions and relations of things can lead us to see what we *ought* to desire. Some examples will aid in the elucidation of these questions.

Suppose we discover that our roof leaks and set about to remedy the difficulty. The example is perfectly in accord with Dewey's approach; value problems arise *wherever* action is called for and it is clear that there are alternative courses of action. We are not confined to what might normally be called "moral" situations. Let us further suppose that intelligent analysis of the situation shows that we have several ways of dealing with the problem; what we want is the "best" way of fixing the defect, or at least a way which is better than other ways. There is no doubt that by taking into account such factors as cost, convenience, and the like, scientific knowledge of the materials and tools will lead us to the best way for resolving the problem. Suppose a second case, one more closely related to human concerns. A man discovers that people shun him because he rarely keeps appointments on time and then becomes angry when he is chided for his lack of punctuality. If that man should desire to change his ways he might ask, What is the best way to overcome these difficulties and to regain the favor and good graces of my friends? Here again it seems fairly obvious that finding the "best" way to proceed is simply a matter of attending to the facts of the situation. The case may be too trivial for us to use the term "scientific knowledge," but it seems fairly clear that no profound moral insight or knowledge from on high is needed in order to resolve the problem. The "best" way to achieve the end desired is dictated by the facts of human psychology. Although this second case is actually more problematic than the first, we may allow that in both examples the best way of proceeding is revealed through knowledge of the various factors in the situation.

Suppose another case involving more obviously ethical issues. A parent desires the good for her child and vows that she will be guided in all her actions by what is genuinely good for the child and not merely by her own prejudices and predilections. Now it seems clear that this vow itself as an end in view — the declared intention to seek for nothing but the good of the child—cannot be discovered merely by objective knowledge of any situation. That any course of action which follows from the initial vow represents the "best" way of acting cannot be discovered merely by appealing to the facts of human psychology, the arrangement of society, and similar sources of knowledge. The initial vow expresses an end, a goal which is good in itself; such a goal sustains itself by its own nature and does not require support from the value of any further consequences. Suppose we allow that seeking the good of the child is a good or desirable goal; the immediate question is: Is it possible to discover the best *means* of realizing that goal through the sort of knowledge which Dewey had in mind? That scientific knowledge can tell us a great deal about human life, its relation to the environment, and its social character cannot be denied. Science, however, is always dependent upon facts that are finished and done with; it draws its life from the accurate representation and explanation of what has taken place. But we do not discover ideal goods — even the general idea that we should strive for the good of the child apart from our selfish predilections — merely by investigating what has happened in the past. The child, moreover, has freedom and entertains ideas about his or her own nature and destiny; there is more than one ideal of fulfillment, and those that have been proposed in the past have not always been consistent with each other. The facts of human psychology and sociology will tell us much about human behavior, and what Dewey liked to call the results of experienced objects, but all by itself and without the intervention of *comprehensive* ideals touching on the proper vocation of man in the world, that knowledge will not suffice. And yet Dewey persistently maintained the opposite thesis; for him scientific knowledge was to be our guide not only in the discovery of means to ends previously agreed upon, but in the determination of ends themselves, which are supposed to be genuine values because they are approved on reflection and are rooted in empirical knowledge.

Dewey seems not to have seen that it is only in relatively simple situations that their problematic character is revealed on the basis of so-called factual analyses alone. The leaky roof has a way of making itself known and to know that we have a problem on our hands requires no extended diagnosis. But there is a formidable gap between a situation of that simplicity and the sort of problem which arises in connection with, for example, the divided self prevented from affirming itself by insufficient courage, or with the conflict between personal honesty and the goal of worldly success. In those cases the "problem" does not announce itself as it does when a physical system goes out of order; instead we require a standard of excellence by reference to which we can say that the situation is not as it ought to be. It is curious that the closer we come to situations which would normally be regarded as "moral" situations, the more difficult it is to see that their problematic character can be discovered merely by scientific analysis.

On Dewey's own view, the determination of means is not independent of ends, of exactly what we ought to desire and hope to achieve. But Dewey also held that the framing of ends in view taken as the proposed resolution of problematic situations depends on the tracing out of means for arriving at these ends. It is difficult to see how a vicious circle is to be avoided. We do not discover the "problematic" character of moral situations merely by analyzing the facts; to be problematic such situations must fall short of an ideal or lack a feature which would complete them. Unless we already know what ends we want to achieve, an analysis of the factual structure of a situation will not itself suffice for diagnosis. It will not do to say that only those desires or ends in view which are framed in accordance with scientific knowledge of means are genuine, because we cannot begin to consider means until we have some idea of where we want to go. Dewey did not see the relevance of goals that emerge not from the scientific appraisal of situations but out of ideal visions portraying what man and society may become. Such ideals can actually be found in his own accounts of the individual, of freedom, and of the ideal society. But it seems clear that these ends were not arrived at as a result of a scientific analysis purporting to disclose the "problematic" character of situations. Instrumentalism is, as the name implies, a philosophy of instruments; instruments, however, are not ends and without ends there can be no appraisal.

Despite the difficulties which Dewey's theory must face, we cannot afford to ignore the fact that it does express a belief held by large numbers of people over recent decades. We are faced, moreover, with a recent upsurge of faith in the power of science to save us; it is therefore imperative that we make a sympathetic attempt to understand what Dewey wanted to say even if there are grounds for holding that it is not wholly true. No one believed more completely in the importance of science for human life and no one made greater claims for it. One of the most reliable clues to the true status of science in American culture is the strength of the belief that science can be made to do at one stroke the work traditionally performed by ethics and religion. Dewey shared that belief.

Dewey believed that the key to connecting science and value lies in the reinterpretation of means and ends in such a way that the two form a continuous process. Dewey distinguishes at the outset between *prizing* and *appraising* (both meanings are sometimes included in his other terms "valuation" and "value"). To prize something — an object, a person, a type of character, a state of affairs — is to hold it as precious, to regard it highly, to honor it. Prizing has a necessary connection with the *personal* aspect of things since it represents an immediate expression of an individual's own values. Appraising means the assigning of value and this involves critical comparison. To appraise is to express the relations between things; appraising is not an immediate response. In perfect accord with the recurring pattern of Dewey's thought, the distinction reflects the difference between an expression which is immediate and emotional — prizing — and one which is predominantly intellectual or reflective in character — appraising. The question which arises is: How are the two related to each other and are both involved equally in valuation?

Dewey did not hesitate to connect value, in the sense of prizing, with human interest and desire. He accepted this much as least of the utilitarian tradition in value theory. But he objected strongly to the identification of desire with private feelings unconnected with behavior and the public interactions between things. Nor would he allow that interest is something which exists independently of an ordered system of desires and concerns. On the contrary, he rejected the widely received opinion that value is "any object of any interest" on the ground that it placed all interests on the same level and leads us to consider them in isolation from each other. He aimed at giving a more subtle account of value in terms of interest and desire, hoping to avoid the subjectivism of previous theories, and at the same time to maintain the continuity between valuation and science.

That people do prize things is taken by Dewey as the primary fact and initial subject matter for all discussion about values. Prizing, however, is not the end of the story; it is but the beginning. The critical problem arises when we attempt to say that some acts of prizing are *better* than others. Some of the things people hold dear are not really worthy of our esteem. As soon as this point is acknowledged it is clear that some standard beyond that of prizing is required. Valuation in the critical sense enters; the critical appraisal of what is prized takes us to the center of the valuation problem. The essence of Dewey's position is found in his attempt to show that these critical evaluations are subject to empirical knowledge and that they involve ends no less than means.

The difference between statements of fact such as "Mt. McKinley is more than 5,000 feet high" or "Kant died in 1804" and appraisal statements such as "this grade of cloth is worth $15 a yard" is that the former express what is already accomplished or completed, whereas the latter lays down a condition for future action. The cloth, according to this view, does not now possess some mysterious property of being "worth" such and such; rather the statement refers to a condition which someone either buying or selling the cloth must conform to in calculating its value. It expresses a condition *to be* met; it is not a record of a datum completed. A norm for Dewey is always a condition of this kind and norms figure in all activity. The important question is whether they state merely custom and convention or whether they set forth relations between things based on empirical grounds which can be traced out in the experience of everybody. Critical appraisals express what is "called for" or what is requisite, what is proper or what is necessary, if one is to have a better (or best) way of proceeding in order to accomplish some end.

Dewey was uneasy over the possibility that the foregoing way of describing appraisals still leaves them in the order of means. If we know what ends we want to achieve, knowledge of the conditions and outcomes of things will lead us to judge the various *means* at our disposal and to declare that one is better than another. If we are to levy taxes, then we must appraise real estate in a certain way; if we want to build a bridge that will safely accommodate a specified volume of traffic in a given time, then we must choose certain ways of operating over others and in so doing we shall say that the needed means are the "proper" or better means. But we seem to be still in the sphere of means. What becomes of ends? Are they to be left outside of the process of critical appraisal? Dewey's answer was unequivocal: No. If we rightly understand the connection between ends and means we shall see that we cannot in fact avoid appraising ends when we evaluate means. The key idea is that science and the method of intelligence become essential to the framing of valuable ends as soon as we see that both are involved in choosing means, and choosing means inevitably forces us into the critical consideration of ends.

This is, in outline, Dewey's solution to the problem of relating knowledge and the method of intelligence to ideal goods and goals. What still remains to be seen is exactly how ends are framed and furnished with critical grounding. Dewey was ready to admit that prizing often means the setting forth of ends and that appraisal, in the sense of specifying conditions to be met, is essentially a matter of judging means. But he tried to show that the separation of ends from consideration of the means whereby they can be attained leads to several undesirable consequences. He was particularly critical of the notion of intrinsic ends, goals "good in themselves" and the like, because it appeared that such notions carry with them the belief in ends supposedly independent of the means to be used for attaining them. He claimed, moreover, that the framing and contemplation of ends apart from

concrete plans and devices for realizing them invariably result in surrendering choices and actual behavior to the impulse of the moment. Energy spent in contemplation of values
severed from natural processes is energy diverted from use
in attending to the matter at hand. When action finally does
become imperative, no preparation has been made, concrete
courses of action have been ignored, and nothing is left but
impulse or habit as the guide for conduct. Dewey's answer to
the problem is to point out that an end is the same as an
occurrence which comes at the end of some process; it is to
be understood in terms of the conditions which bring it to
pass. The idea which we have of that end — the end "in view"
— cannot be independent of the means or the conditions
through which it comes about. Dewey's claim is that this
idea is "warranted" only to the extent to which it has actually
been framed in accordance with actual means. The upshot of
the position is that ideals or ends which we are unable to
support with actual means of realization turn out to be "mere"
ideals — the result of whim or fancy. The difficulty remaining,
however, concerns the relative merits of different ends. Our
ability to show that a given interest or desire has been framed
in accordance with the conditions needed to realize it does
not automatically "warrant" that end. A goal is not good
merely because it can be reached.

Dewey was confident that this and other objections could
be met through an adequate understanding of the continuity
between means and ends. His case finally rests on that conception. Citing the classic essay of Charles Lamb on the origin
of roast pork, Dewey began his attack on the belief that one
can view and value ends apart from the means used to obtain
them. In that story, it will be remembered, the author told
how a house containing some pigs had burned down and how
the owners searching in the ruins touched the roasted pigs,

burned their fingers and then, automatically touching them to their lips, discovered to their great surprise the delicious taste of roast pork. Acting upon their new discovery, they gathered other pigs, confined them to a house, set it on fire and thus produced more excellent roasts. Dewey rejoiced in this story because it illustrated his point that no end has its value entirely apart from the means used to reach it. The enjoyment of roast pork is immediate and it seems to have this value all by itself and without regard to any other fact. Further thought, however, will suggest that we may cease to enjoy it if it can be produced only by so crude and wasteful a process. He questioned the value of an enjoyment which sustains itself only if we do not consider the way in which it comes about. Means have a being of their own; they are not confined to producing just the end we have in view and no more. The use of means always leads to several results and to a plurality of ends. Dewey objected to the singling out of just one item as *the* end. The roast pigs represent but one result of the burnt house and even if we adopted that method with the sole aim of producing roast pork, we could not avoid producing other consequences at the same time. The *end* we had in view has, therefore, to be considered in relation to the *many ends* which the means will produce. Means and ends are never independent of each other.

We can draw together the many strands of Dewey's argument by viewing his position from a distance. He sees that scientific knowledge is best fitted to reveal the natures and tendencies of things; it is most adequate to teach us what is likely to happen if we follow certain courses of action. He admits in effect that the method of intelligence gives us our clearest guidance with regard to means. He will not admit that its guidance is limited to knowledge of means. He wants

to show that it can and should have some constraining effect
on the rise and formation of desires, or ends in view. He
achieves his result by connecting means with ends. No end
as an actual result is disconnected from some process — means
— whereby it is attained. In a given case of intelligent or
directed action, there must be some end in view, some goal
desired which it is the function of the means to achieve. But
though there be one end in view, no means is ever confined
to the production of one end; in all processes there are many
ends in the sense of many results. It is therefore impossible
for the end in view to stand all alone; it is but one result
besides others and it is singled out for special attention because it was "the" end we had before us guiding our activity.
In estimating its value, we must take into account the other
results which our means will carry along with them. Roast
pork we may desire and enjoy; having it for dinner represents
an end which is valued. But our question is: Can we still
continue to appraise that end as good and valuable if we
take into account all the other "ends" that must also be
reckoned with when we use the house-burning method? This
is not to say that we cannot find another method; it is to say
that consideration of the consequences of the method entered
into the process of evaluating the end itself. Our enjoyment
of the pork is transformed by the thought of the house de-
stroyed.

More important than the final success or failure of Dewey's
theory are the implications his attempt to synthesize knowledge and evaluation have had for American life. His approach furnishes us with at least three insights into the
American character. First, action and practical intelligence
take precedence over all forms of contemplation and speculation; secondly, ideal goals are not "starry-eyed" projections of
human desire but rather visions of improvement rooted in the

actual possibilities of situations; and thirdly, value comes to be taken out of the sphere of the individual and personal and relocated in social progress and in the struggle to eliminate the ills of political, economic, and social life. A common theme runs through each of these characteristics; all thought and concern must be focused by the problems arising from the contemporary social situation. If life is essentially a struggle, it is a struggle against *present* problems in the environment. When human energy is directed either to the contemplation of the past for its own sake or to reveling in the attractions of mere ideals and visions of other worlds, it is energy misplaced. The precarious nature of life hedges us in from birth to death; we can survive and improve our lot only insofar as we succeed in focusing our energies on the actual problems before us. We can hope to solve them if we can locate them, discover the best way to attack them, carry through our plans while at the same time avoiding the distractions of long-range speculation. This is Dewey's vision of the function of intelligence in the modern world; it is the essence of practicality. Mistrust of abstractions and speculations has permeated American life and culture in the first half of the twentieth century. In giving classic expression to that mistrust Dewey rightly deserves the title of *the* American philosopher in our time.

We would do grave injustice to Dewey's comprehensive philosophy if we omitted his treatment of art and of the aesthetic in man's experience. The pragmatists, and not least Dewey himself, were often criticized for emphasizing only the surface of life, the immediate and the practical, the material and the mundane, neglecting the loftier dimensions of man's life and experience. Unlike James, Dewey did not have an intimate sense of the transcendent ideal from which religion draws its life, although his *Common Faith* proved to be a most provocative book on the subject. Ideal meaning for Dewey was centered not in religion but in art. His interpretation of the aesthetic dimension furnishes evidence of a trend found in many thinkers of the twentieth century. We may describe this trend in the following way: Religion has fallen on evil days, the great moral traditions of Western civilization have been brought into question; science, progress, and the possibilities of history have been made to take their place. But for many this has not been enough. Is there, they have asked, no source of meaning for life which takes us beyond the struggle for existence? Is the whole of life to be summed up in the effort to master ourselves and our surroundings? There are those who have seen the point of these questions only to submerge them again with the claim that man has no power to answer them. But for others these questions have led to basically aesthetic solutions; the ideal meaning embodied in art has often appeared as the one point where the flatness and monotony of a purely mundane view of things is transcended. We want to go beyond organism and environment, beyond the push and pull of social and political life, to some ideal fulfillment that is more lasting than successful manipulation of things. But for the majority in a skeptical age there is no "going beyond" in religious terms; the one remaining answer short of despair is to be found in art and in aesthetic perception.

We need not enter into the details of Dewey's theory; it is enough to indicate its main drift. Art as *expression,* in an appropriate medium, of those interests and delights that fascinate us must not be isolated from experience. We must exercise care not to ignore the origin of art in ordinary life. What Dewey called the museum conception of art is to be rejected as unworthy on both counts; it isolates art from experience through the idea that art is "spiritual" and has nothing to do with "material" things, and it severs the connection between artistic production and ordinary events of aesthetic interest by setting it up on a pedestal. Dewey argued instead for an understanding of art which sees it as a direct development stemming from aesthetic perception; art results from experience and, in a certain sense, *is* experience. It is experience in that heightened sense in which experience becomes valuable for its own sake. Although art means primarily a making, and is thus a purposeful product, it is also the channel whereby we pass beyond the relentless task of solving problems in an endless chain. Art helps to deliver us from the endlessness of means and ends situations by pointing up experiences which have completion in them; they are valuable in themselves and do not drive us on to the never ending series of problems and solutions.

It is important to notice that Dewey's plea for connecting art with the aesthetic aspect of experience and with ordinary life does not mean merely spreading art among the "masses." It especially does not mean the perpetuation of the museum conception by extending it to more and more people. Dewey was striving for a new understanding of the nature of art so that as opportunities for viewing paintings and hearing music increase, the individual can experience these artistic products as the development and accentuation of familiar experiences valuable in themselves. In this way ordinary life is enriched; it is endowed with a vividness and poignancy which would otherwise be lost.

To ignore the element of aesthetic value in Dewey's vision of human experience is not only to be unjust to the man, but it is also to neglect an important aspect of the American character. American openness to experience, American willingness to participate in the manners and customs of others which is so often mistaken (especially by Europeans) for naïveté, is actually a basic sensitivity to what Dewey called the aesthetic features of life. Delight and wonder, interest and enjoyment, are at the root of the enthusiasm so often found among us, both at home and abroad. This characteristic gives, in the end, the lie to the view which says that American life is "crass," "merely utilitarian," and "materialistic." Without in the least denying that those qualities do exist and have made their presence felt in a powerful way, there remains interest in, and concern for, the enjoyment of experience itself. Dewey detected the existence of this interest and sought to find a place for it within his own vision. The question of our time is whether aesthetic value is enough; whether it can suffice to provide the courage which, in former times, was derived from the faith of religion. Whatever may be the answer to this question it is clear that Dewey went further than is often thought in providing an essentially technological civilization with a humanized view of the world.

V

Alfred North Whitehead: SPECULATIVE

THINKING, SCIENCE, AND EDUCATION

It seems clear enough from our study of American thinkers over the past three-quarters of a century that science has played a major role in the development of their thought. James was trained under the great zoologist, Louis Agassiz, and *The Principles of Psychology* was a pioneer work in a field that was then a new and rapidly growing science. Peirce was familiar with an astounding quantity of scientific research and even carried on some of his own; the "laboratory" spirit, as he called it, pervades his thought. Royce developed his voluntaristic idealism and his belief in the importance of purposive activity partly in response to the challenge presented by the mechanical and purposeless universe supposed to follow from the biology of Darwin. Dewey was both the prophet of science and its high priest; he took science as the standard pattern for all thought and he represented it as a saving force, the one great hope of man in his struggle against nature and the evils of historical life.

A predominantly technological culture such as our own may naturally be expected to take science seriously, and to be aware of the contribution it has made to human well-being. Our philosophers have echoed this awareness. But in the face

161

of our debt to applied science we have at times overemphasized the products which research makes possible, while failing to pay full respect to the pure science behind them.
Despite the imbalance, science in some form has never been
far from the center of American life and thought in the
present century. This fact invites the deepest reflection. A
question which first made itself felt in the 'forties, is being
asked with greater urgency at present despite the new impetus
given to science by the current race for outer space: Has
science any limitations and, if so, what are they and how
shall we try to compensate for them? The concern, in short,
is for a more critical approach to the scientific enterprise and
a more profound scrutiny of its foundations.

At a much earlier time, Royce raised his critical voice
against the sufficiency of science as the final interpreter of
things. James warned against confusing the theoretical standpoint of scientific observation and explanation with the outlook of the self who lives, moves, and has his being in the
world of concrete things. But the tide was against them; the
success of science was obvious and dazzling. There was no
staying its sweep. Besides, Royce was identified with religion
and an idealist philosophy — the supposed natural enemies
of science — and James's practicalism appeared to many theoretical minds as but another form of the "tender-minded"
orientation that he had officially rejected. Neither Royce nor
James could furnish the necessary critical appraisal; another
was called for. The situation demanded someone who combined special scientific competence with philosophical depth.
That man turned out to be Alfred North Whitehead. Trained
in physics and mathematics, and possessed of a remarkably
original speculative power, he was perfectly fitted for the
task of explaining the nature of science, and of interpreting
its proper place in modern life and thought. As can be seen

from his incisive comparison of Dewey's thought with his own, he grasped the demand of the situation at once. Dewey, he said, pays attention to what scientists *do* and I to what they *assume*.

If we are asked to justify the inclusion of Whitehead in a discussion of philosophical thinking in America, the case can readily be made. To ignore his contribution would be to overlook one of the most fruitful interplays between thinker and situation in the history of thought. His coming to America provided the opportunity and stimulus for his most original thinking, and he in turn gave to the American intellectual world a new insight into its own foundation. The frankness and enthusiasm of the American temper appealed to him; the pervading atmosphere seemed to free his thoughts, so that during his life in the United States he was able to give expression to his most comprehensive reflections on science, education, society, civilization, and the place of religion in the cosmic scheme. In the other direction, his philosophy had a decisive role to play on the American scene; only now are we beginning to understand its full import. The striking fact is that there should have been a thinker who could make lasting contributions to logic and the foundations of mathematics and at the same time attempt to explain to his generation the true nature and limitations of scientific thought. Others have attempted to caution against overestimating the powers of science, but rarely could these critics speak from an intimate knowledge of the subject. Whitehead was of a different stamp; he had a clear and profound grasp of the impact made by science on the modern world. He wrote eloquently not only of the history of science but also of the manner in which modern life has been shaped by the scientific outlook. And yet he did not shrink from the task of exposing the abstract character of the cherished results of science and of demanding that these abstractions be brought to the bar of direct experience. American philosophy needed his critical word.

Whitehead's thought embraces both a technical cosmology couched in a language which no layman (and not all philosophers) can understand, and a vision about the importance of modern life and civilization which every intelligent person can follow. For example, in a most intricate doctrine called the method of extensive abstraction, Whitehead developed a way of explaining the connection between concrete experience directly present and the abstract concepts used in natural science for understanding that experience. This doctrine is complex and difficult to grasp. On the other hand, in such books as *Religion in the Making, The Aims of Education,* and *Adventures of Ideas,* he was able to write with an arresting simplicity about matters of the most immediate import. Though cryptic at points, these writings can be read with profit and understanding by the intelligent layman. There is, moreover, an intimate connection between the two aspects of his thought. Whitehead's views on education, the place of science in the modern world, the role of the aesthetic in experience, and the meaning of civilization are all rooted in the doctrines going to make up his philosophy of organism. The former are readily understood while the latter can be comprehended only by the expert. And yet the two aspects are bound up with each other. His attack on compartmentalization in education, for example, follows directly from his theory of abstraction in thought. Studies of selected aspects of experience are founded in abstraction and demand focus of attention; to study *this* we have to ignore *that.* Precise knowledge is always partial. To discover what has been omitted means returning to the direct experience with which we began. The integrity of experience demands that we refuse to settle for abstractions. Another case in point is Whitehead's conception of civilization. His belief that civilization must either advance or face decay depends on the metaphysical principle that reality is always in process. A creative advance means triumphing over a learned orthodoxy through adventure — grappling with present problems in the light of new ideals. Decay sets in when we are content with the perpetuation of a past success and refuse to venture beyond the safe repetition of a well-tried method.

Whitehead's thought is sure to have an increasing influence on American cultural life. That influence will extend to many different aspects of experience. To trace out all the ramifications of his philosophic vision would mean traversing the entire universe. The task would be endless. Happily there is a central feature of his philosophy which happens also to be of major importance for the American scene — the doctrine that all precise thought is abstract and that all systems of scientific explanation presuppose a metaphysical background. This doctrine led Whitehead to expose the limitations of modern science and at the same time demonstrate the inescapable demands of speculative thinking.

Whitehead went beyond pointing out the actual involvement of metaphysical categories and principles in modern scientific thought; he sought to show that the involvement is necessary and that it belongs to the function of reason itself. If clear thought, he argued, is also precise, then it is abstract in the sense that it selects only those features of a situation which are relevant for a given line of thinking. For example, prior to Darwin's time the problems of classifying species were separated sharply from questions as to how a given arrangement of species had come about. The question of development was not considered relevant to the aims of taxonomy and hence was neglected. Though selection inevitably means omission and the suppression of a background deemed irrelevant to the topic singled out for attention, the reflective question is this: To what extent must our understanding of what we have selected be modified in the light of what we have omitted? A very large part of Whitehead's complex philosophical scheme is devoted to answering that question. His answer is that we shall never come to raise the question unless we are aware that omissions have taken place. Once we are sensitive to the problem, our task becomes that of seeking to recover the suppressed background; we must concern ourselves as far as possible with the general features of the whole. In the end the full understanding of science requires both a cosmology and a speculative philosophy devoted to the discovery of the most pervasive categories and general principles of things.

For our purpose we may select three focal points in Whitehead's system. Two points have to do with the abstractness of science and the need for speculative philosophy, while the third directs attention to education and the consequences for teaching at all levels that follow from his attack upon the compartmentalization of knowledge.

Whitehead saw that bodies of knowledge which express the details of things are always dependent upon certain comprehensive ideas that define the general character of the universe of which the details are a part. His knowledge of the history of science taught him that increasing success in mastering details invariably leads to neglect of the general ideas at the base. Thus for a long time the success of the Newtonian scheme directed attention away from the *critical* scrutiny of its general assumptions about the nature of the universe. Such neglect will cause no apparent difficulty over shorter periods of time, since successful explanation and prediction of specific matters of fact and their relationships will seem to guarantee at the same time the validity of the general ideas behind the system. Subsequent developments, however, may show that the supposition is not warranted. Conclusions about detail must in the end be limited by the assumptions contained in the fundamental principles of the system. These principles belong in the end to philosophy, where neither total precision nor certainty is possible. The history of Newtonian physics illustrates the point. It is not, as is sometimes supposed, that modern physics simply nullifies the Newtonian system; it is rather that reflection on the general ideas at its base has revealed its limited applicability. There are phenomena which it does not adequately express, and we are therefore faced with the alternative of denying them in order to save the system or of limiting the range of its validity. Whitehead saw that unless critical attention is paid to the fundamental principles and concepts we shall remain content with a knowledge of detail the true limitations of which are not known. We need the reflecting or philosophic mind as well as the analytic or scientific mind if we are to escape dogmatism and provincialism.

The Baconian ideal of science according to which all generalization is but a short-hand expression of particular, brute fact runs counter to the position Whitehead defends. In Bacon we can never get beyond particular fact; all systematic construction is supposed to be but a more convenient way of expressing the details so far collected. What Bacon failed to see is that the enterprise of collecting data itself rests on assumptions as to what is to count as a datum, and that, in any case, the collection and classification of data cannot suffice to answer the questions of explanation that science ultimately raises. The point is that general principles of various sorts are present at the outset; they are not merely subsequent to the enumeration and description of particular cases.

Before we can apprehend particular matter of fact, we must knew in a general way what we are after, we must concentrate attention and ignore what we regard as irrelevant to our purpose. Science means delimitation and selection; the guidance of general principles is always required. But these principles themselves, just because they are intended to guide a specialized inquiry, will be partial and limited to the enterprise at hand. We are constantly in need of the reflective and critical mind if we are not to be seduced into taking such principles as a total and final truth. "One aim of philosophy," wrote Whitehead, "is to challenge the half-truths constituting the scientific first principles" (*Process and Reality*, p. 15).

The scientist, moreover, will find himself assuming the language and the general ideas which form the intellectual climate of his age. Whether he regards the primary datum as the representation of a fixed, identical, and enduring object or as a series of events linked in a process will make a great deal of difference in the final reckoning, no matter how irrelevant the distinction may appear to a mind concentrating on the mere recording of immediate detail. A given investigator, for example, working at a particular time will find himself subject to at least two sorts of intellectual control. On the one hand, his immediate focus of attention will be guided and constrained by ideas expressing the nature of the particular problem on which he is working. His activity as an investigator doing *that* particular piece of work will be subject to the control of the hypothesis under examination. This part of his consciousness will be clear and, insofar as the immediate focus of attention is concerned, he will be able to say what he is doing. But that focus does not exhaust his intellectual make-up; in addition he will have, as a more or less unconscious part of his outlook, the dominant assumptions of his period concerning the basic nature of his enterprise. He may, for example, be working on the assumption — vague, diffused, and not clearly grasped in its implications — that his task is that of seeing every phenomenon in atomistic fashion because each phenomenon is what it is apart from all else in the universe.

Suppose, on the other hand, another investigator working on the assumption that just the opposite is the real task of inquiry, namely, that the phenomenon is known only insofar as it is grasped within a network of connections with other things. The fundamentally different outlooks will surely lead to significant differences of interpretation when we seek to give an organic or comprehensive account of the universe and our experience, even though we may try to ignore those differences for short-run and immediate purposes. There is the possibility of showing that the "data" in both cases will be the same regardless of the fundamental assumptions of the investigator. And, we can usually abstract from the concrete situation to an extent sufficient to warrant the claim. But we cannot ignore the differences in outlook when we seek to pass beyond short-run and hypothetical interpretations. For not only will the nature of a special science such as biology be dependent upon our answers to questions about its aims and the type of explanation it seeks, but larger questions such as the place of science in a civilization, the nature of education, the relation of science to religion and to art, will all be different depending on whether we take the atomistic point of view of the first investigator or the organic one of the second.

Whitehead saw clearly our common tendency (not confined to students of natural science) to ignore the most fundamental, the dimly conscious and always vague, assumptions which define the "climate of opinion" of an epoch. He understood how easy it is to confuse the fact that these principles are on the fringe of consciousness and do not appear to determine our thinking with the very different claim that they make no difference and can safely be left out of account. He tried to show that not only do first principles change from epoch to epoch, a fact which accounts for different philosophies and climates of opinion, but also that the existence of these first principles, ill understood as they may be, plays an essential role in the gaining of knowledge. Newton, for example, though primarily a man of science, was determined in his scientific thought by the philosophical assumptions of his time. His supposition that the natural object can be thought of as an *instantaneous* configuration of material led to neglect of the temporal element in the explanation of a thing. This neglect led in turn to the imposition of fundamental limits on the validity of his scheme. Whitehead's oft-repeated point was that reflection on first principles — speculative philosophy — is not a harmless luxury which we may indulge in or ignore as we see fit; it is an enterprise which we neglect at our peril.

Closely related to Whitehead's insistence on the need for reflective thinking was his criticism of the partial character of scientific knowledge. He expressed this point in several ways: sometimes he called attention to the mistake of isolating a datum and of supposing that its meaning is independent of the universe to which it belongs. At other points he spoke, in his own formidable language, of the "fallacy of misplaced concreteness," by which he meant the reduction of the concrete fact to but one of its features, usually a feature capable of expression in very precise or quantitative form. The spatial character of things, for example, has its own status in the constitution of the total fact, but we must not yield to the temptation to regard it as better founded in reality than the more immediate and aesthetic features of the fact. That a fact is arresting or poignant belongs to it as fully as its occupancy of space. All aspects of reality are equally "real"; not all are equally important.

At still other times Whitehead made his point about the necessarily abstract character of all precise knowledge by analyzing the nature of precision itself. Precision in thought means having tight control over the application of concepts and reducing vagueness to a minimum. For these purposes our attention must be concentrated and our expression of just those features of reality we have selected for study must be rigorous. Precision means abstraction and isolation; in order to achieve precision in thought we must abstract the object from everything which is not the object and we must treat the object as if it were all by itself. Isolation means ignoring the habitat of a thing and regarding it as having its being and significance apart from the qualities and relations from which it is abstracted. Wherever we have precision we run the risk of ignoring as irrelevant what might prove fatal to our results if we were forced to take it into account.

It might appear that Whitehead was an opponent of science and of precise thought, preferring instead some form of immediate insight or intuition. The truth is far otherwise. Not only did he pay close attention to the conditions under which abstractions are well founded, but he saw better than any other modern thinker both the need for analytic precision and the inevitable abstraction which goes along with it. Previous thinkers had directed attention to the problem of preserving the integrity of direct experience in the face of scientific analysis and explanation, but they were often tempted to adopt romantic solutions which meant a denial of scientific knowledge in the end. Others ignored the underlying issue altogether on the grounds that analysis exhausts the work of the intellect and that the supposed need to preserve the unity of experience is no more than a pseudo-problem. Whitehead's view was more subtle. He understood that the precision of scientific analysis must result in the dismembering of what initially comes to us as one whole. He was sensitive to the charge advanced by poets and philosophers that qualities and values encountered in direct experience vanish when that same experience is expressed and explained through the concepts and language of the exact sciences. On the other hand, Whitehead, as a mathematician and scientist himself, was equally alive to the demands of analytic precision. To obtain knowledge we must analyze and make use of abstract ideas. Unless we are prepared to engage in theoretical interpretation of a sort which takes us far beyond the contours of things directly presented to our senses, we can have no science. Whitehead was unwilling to ignore the demand of either side; he sought to show that we must preserve both direct experience and theoretical interpretation. The key to his solution is found in the way he sought to relate one to the other.

All knowing sets out from and finally must return to the concrete world of direct experience. Scientific knowledge is by nature abstract and partial, but not all abstractions are objectionable. There are well-founded abstractions which survive the test of being confronted with the concrete experience from which they arise. But the degree and import of an abstraction can be estimated only if we attend to the concrete situation in immediate experience. We need, in short, to pay attention to the general features of the universe as well as to the details which the abstractions express. If we attend to the whole we can engage in abstract thought with the confidence that we have some safeguard against vicious abstractions. To provide that safeguard is a major task of speculative thought which, contrary to popular opinion, is always rooted in concrete experience. Speculative thinking has two tasks: to discover by attending to direct experience what has been omitted or left out of account by the abstracting intellect, and to express the unity of that experience by discovering the pervasive categories exemplified throughout the whole universe. When we know, for example, the proper relations between number and quality or between causal relation and the purposive behavior of things, we are in a position to connect and unify what would otherwise appear as a heap of atomic facts. Direct experience is unified and continuous, but by itself it yields no theoretical knowledge; the abstracting intellect leads to such knowledge, but it does so at the price of ignoring some features of things and of destroying the integrity of direct experience. It was Whitehead's contention that only a renewal of speculative thinking can show us the way to integrate the two aspects of intelligent life.

Whitehead would have made a vital contribution if he had done no more than cause us to consider afresh the need for speculative thinking in an age of science. But he went further; he went on to relate his doctrines to other regions of contemporary life and civilization. Among other topics, he focused on the meaning of education. He sought to point out the consequences for the educational adventure that follow from the indispensability of science on the one hand and the need to criticize its partiality and abstractness on the other. Whitehead's little book *The Aims of Education* is one of the most important pieces written on the subject in our century. This is true chiefly because it not only pays attention to the structure of education at large but aims at understanding the proper place of scientific instruction in the total curriculum as well. The problem of understanding the impact of science in the modern world has its parallel in the school and university. The educational curriculum is a mirror of the universe; just as we seek to estimate how much science grasps and how much it misses of man's total experience, so we must ask about the place of science and the importance to be given it in the entire course of study. Whitehead was in a most favorable position for dealing with such questions because he possessed a comprehensive theory of both experience and the cosmos. Here, as in other instances, his philosophical vision was the guiding factor in the treatment of the most urgent human problems.

"A merely well informed man," Whitehead wrote, "is the most useless bore on God's earth." This comment furnishes an initial clue to his approach to education. He opposed the prevalent belief that the mind is a passive thing to be "filled" with a supply of information through the classroom. On the contrary, for him "inert ideas" are worth next to nothing; the educated man is one who knows how to reflect on ideas, how to test them, how to apply them in concrete situations, and how to relate them to many regions of life and experience. The educated man does not merely repeat what he has learned; he is able to create something new through the rearrangement of ideas. Moreover, the information and ideas received through the school must be utilized. Education is aimed at the development of understanding and it must include training the young in the art of utilizing knowledge. The person himself must actively relate what has been given him by his teachers to his own plans and purposes, his hopes and fears, desires and needs. Whitehead had grave doubts about the value of "knowledge for its own sake"; he argued instead that all learning must be directed to what he called "the insistent present" and that it must be focused on the dominant problems of the age in which the student lives.

Nothing could be closer or more germane to the American concept of education. Learning should point to current issues; ideas must have a "cutting edge." Knowledge of what has been, important though it is, must not be pursued for its own sake; its value lies in bringing forth understanding which is both in and for the present. Whitehead was opposed to the undervaluing of the present in favor of glorifying the past; in his view the present embraces both past and future because it has temporal "thickness." We come here upon a striking example of the connection between Whitehead's metaphysics and his educational ideas. The present is not a mere "now" or point which is without duration or temporal breadth; the present has a "spread" in it in the sense that it contains the dying edge of the past or fleeting reality and the growing edge of the future or creative reality. The present, like Janus, faces in two directions at once. Following in the footsteps of Bergson, Whitehead saw the error in any theory which takes temporal development as the mere succession of instants which are in themselves essentially timeless because they are without "breadth" and represent no time at all. He held, on the contrary, that time may be divided into parts if such parts represent durations or portions of time. A *present* time therefore cannot be a bare instant but must contain within its own breadth the edges of the past and the future.

This way of viewing the present has important consequences for education. The present is the matrix of all life and thought; it is the time in which we are forced to live and it contains the issues which everyman must confront. Because the present is not a static reality, however, it is not conveniently waiting to be analyzed as if it were some relic of a distant and frozen past. The present is a dynamic affair; it is the place where past and future converge, and as the growing edge of things it is always involved in change. To grasp the problems of present life we must look both to the past and to the future.

To live in the present and grapple with its issues requires

that we know the backgrounds and antecedents of current problems. Critical study of the past, then, has some point; without it we cannot fully understand the present ground on which we stand. The future, on the other hand, is no less involved. A changing reality has a *direction* as it plunges into the future; what has been is but a prelude to what is to be. One of the basic tasks of education is to inculcate some feel for this fluid nature of the present and to develop the art of judgment in using knowledge so as to help shape the future course of events. The idea of influencing the future brings us to another of Whitehead's basic topics — the utilization of learning.

"Education is the acquisition of the art of the utilization of knowledge." This text expresses in succinct form much that is central to Whitehead's vision. To expound it fully would take us to such topics as the relation between theoretical concepts and practical applications, the place of mathematics and the natural sciences in the course of study, the role of the teacher and the obligations of students in the venture of learning. There is too much to be considered in brief compass; paying some attention to the basic idea will, nevertheless, repay the effort.

The term "utilization" has a pragmatic overtone; it reminds us of the doctrine that all knowledge is to be instrumental and that its validity is strictly a function of problem-solving and success in achieving ends. The identification is far from exact; Whitehead was too much of a Platonist to be comfortable in the camp of pragmatism. Unlike Dewey, he was wary of the belief that proving an idea and utilizing it are internally connected. Proof is accomplished either by experience or logic, or both, whereas utilization belongs to what we do with the ideas proved in the resolution of current problems or the enhancement of life. Whitehead was ready to acknowledge the connection between the practical interests of a thinker and the rational processes in his life, but he was uneasy over what he took to be the pragmatic theory of truth. Interest stimulates thought at the beginning and in the end we must return to the bearing of an idea on our own plans and purposes. But the process of rational support has its own integrity and is not dependent upon our interests. We do not bother to seek for the proof of an idea unless it first seems worthy of attention and concern. And after we have found intellectual support for the idea we seek to appropriate it and discover its import in human life. Interest and utilization are important, but intellectual processes of testing and justification retain their autonomy.

By "utilization" Whitehead did not mean the instrumental function of changing the external situation; he meant rather the creative response of the individual, his ability to relate an idea to other ideas, to other experiences, and finally to the dominant interests of his life. Utilization is an art because there is no clear formula which can tell us how to do it. The teacher can instruct directly and sharpen the mind; he can impart information and he can develop skill in intellectual operations. But understanding and the art of utilization cannot be thus inculcated; both belong to the creative province of art. Success in the attainment of an art demands the utmost co-operation between teacher and student.

If education is to have as its basic aim the utilization of knowledge in life, we shall have to pay close attention to exactly what knowledge we have in mind, and how the various subject matters are to be organized so as to form a course of study. With regard to a practical question of this sort we find once again the closest possible connection between Whitehead's general metaphysics and his theory of education. His concern for the integrity of experience and his doctrine that all precise knowledge is abstract and partial stand behind his insistence that we must do away with "the fatal disconnection of subjects which kills the vitality of our modern curriculum." If life and knowledge are to be integrated, knowledge and education must reflect this unity. Whitehead sought ways of avoiding the twin evils to which every course of study is exposed: the array of empty, even if exciting, generalizations which give the student a false sense of mastery of a field, and the myopic attention to detail which results in loss of understanding of a field as a whole and of its place in relation to other fields of study. The strategy dictated by Whitehead's general theory of experience is clear; generalizations are essential but they must be seen through and by means of the details since it is the details they connect. Understanding as the ultimate aim of education means the discovery of the general truth, but such truth has to be rooted in particular fact; without such an anchorage the general truth is empty. Knowledge of detail, on the other hand, is equally empty unless the import of particular fact is understood in relation both to general truth and some picture of the whole universe.

The unifying feature of education is Life — the basic reality for the philosophy of organism. Life has unity and integrity, and it needs both to sustain itself. Knowledge, however, is plural; there are many subjects and sciences. The major problem is to show how the many subjects are interrelated so as to mirror the unity of life and make the proper utilization of knowledge possible. Every subject expresses some feature or aspect of our life and world; if each subject is left in isolation from every other there is no way of showing how the particular feature it expresses is related to other features, nor can we understand how the many aspects of things go together to make up the one life we live and the one world we encounter. The result of isolation is that each subject of study becomes a self-contained entity from which, as Whitehead put it, "nothing follows." To counteract this result we must understand that each subject matter in the curriculum represents but one aspect of things; the total or integrated picture calls for the interrelation of the many facets into which our direct experience has been analyzed. Just as the one ray of light can be broken up so as to reveal a spectrum of colors, the unity of life is divided by analytic understanding into the many studies — mathematics, natural and social sciences, literature, languages, philosophy, history — which are familiar to all as the standard content of instruction. The main task of education is to reconstitute the unity of life and experience by seeking to express the interconnections between the different subject matters. Education is not to be a heap of subjects, but rather a spectrum of topics each of which is a reflection of and commentary on life.

Whitehead's contention from the beginning to the end of his thought is that while theoretical knowledge of things can be achieved only by analyzing and abstracting, selecting and omitting, the unity of life and experience can be restored only through the constructive activity of speculative thought. In the end there must be synthesis and reconstruction; the results of precise thought must be so related that their bearing on present life becomes clear. Education is a test case; it means the introducing of the young to the nature and meaning of life through the medium of the many subject matters. If the various subjects of instruction are presented as no more than a series of disconnected and self-contained curiosities, the integrity of life and experience will be lost and in the end even the particular subjects themselves will lose their meaning. For it is not true that study of a particular subject can be sustained without some purpose in view. The reason why we consider any subject worth studying always takes us beyond that subject; reflection shows that devoted study of any topic is made possible by some conviction concerning the purpose and contribution of that subject in a comprehensive scheme of things. Fragmentation in education can be overcome only by a common focus or reference point. Whitehead found this focus in *life* expressing itself in the present. This conclusion, though suggested by reflection on the nature of education, has deep roots in Whitehead's philosophy of organism.

Let us consider the meaning we are to attach to Whitehead's claim that the various subject matters of instruction must be related to each other and to present life. In view of the current importance of the place of exact science in the course of study, there is considerable point in singling out mathematics as an example. Whitehead distinguished between the type and amount of mathematics demanded of a student planning to specialize in the field and that demanded of the general liberal arts student. In either case the subject must be presented in a way which eliminates the popular notion of mathematics as a recondite subject. For Whitehead, mathematics meant chiefly the study of abstract ideas, general ideas, that is, and regular relations which concern number, quantity, and space. These relations are ingredient in the world and, though capable of abstract treatment, they are not to be thought of as existing merely in a world apart.* Pure or applied, however, the important thing about the study of mathematics is to grasp the general ideas. Whitehead severely criticized the multiplication of problems and the learning of theorems in any branch of mathematics if the result is neglect of the basic ideas involved. The problem set should illustrate these ideas and students should not be taught to perform operations without under-

* One of Whitehead's important historical insights was that Greek mathematics failed to be more fruitful in mastering the world precisely because Greek thinkers overemphasized the fact that abstract relations are separable from things and can be studied in their own right.

standing the ideas behind them. The learning of special theorems should be curtailed in the interest of presenting the general methods by which they be obtained. Unless the general is emphasized in the teaching of the subject, the important role of mathematics in showing the student how to handle abstract ideas will be lost. It is some comfort to note that the recent revolution in the teaching of mathematics throughout the schools of America follows Whitehead's suggestions closely.

A second point of fundamental importance has to do with our tendency to equate mathematics with *quantity*. This identification has led to a traditional suspicion of mathematics on the ground that quantitative explanation destroys the qualities of things. Whitehead resisted this conclusion. His studies in the foundations of mathematics and the historic work with Bertrand Russell that led to *Principia Mathematica* went far in the direction of recovering the truth, held fast by the ancient Platonic tradition, that mathematics is essentially a matter of relations and proportions. Quantity and measurement have their place, but they do not define the field of mathematics. Relations, proportions, and harmonies are the proper concern of mathematics. Whitehead expressed the point well in his arresting essay, "Mathematics and the Good," when he wrote: "mathematics is the general science of Pattern." Quantification and number represent special aspects of that general science, but they do not exhaust it. It is clear, moreover, that the value to be derived from the study of mathematics in the liberal arts curriculum comes from its treatment of the general relatedness of things, and from its treatment of abstract ideas in accordance with a rigorous logical method.

In our enthusiasm to correct an ancient error, we must not go to the opposite extreme and underestimate the aspect of quantity. It is there as a pervasive feature of our world, a fact well known to the ancient Pythagoreans who were fond of saying that all things are made out of numbers. Whitehead was thoroughly aware of this fact; it is behind his emphasis on the relevance of quantity to things not normally thought to have anything to do with it. "You cannot evade quantity," he wrote. "You may fly to poetry and to music and quantity and number will face you in your rhythms and your octaves." Even in questions of historical interpretation and evaluation we find ourselves confronted with quantity. If we say, for example, that one composer had a large influence upon another, we find it difficult to avoid asking, "How large?" and we attempt to answer our question by some indication of degree or extent. Our belief in the importance of quantity is deeply founded. Whitehead did not mean to deny this importance; he objected rather to the idea that because number can be treated in abstraction from actual things and instances, arithmetic and algebra may therefore be taught as if they had nothing whatever to do with concrete objects and events. It seemed to him that the purpose of the liberal arts curriculum could best be served by showing the connections between mathematics and concrete experience. The aim is not to point up the importance of mathematics for non-mathematicians by showing that it has valuable technological applications, but rather to destroy the popular belief that mathematics is "recondite" — that it exists only in a world apart, a study to be viewed with awe and then promptly ignored. If, however, mathematics is, as Whitehead believed, the study of the general patterns of things, it must prove in the end to have an intimate connection with everyday life.

When we consider those who have made important contributions to educational theory we tend to associate their names with some one dominant idea. The name of Dewey, for example, calls to mind the idea that interest and learning are intimately connected with each other and that formal education must remain continuous with ordinary living experience. When we think of Plato, we are led at once to the idea that education is an extended process of self-knowledge undergirding the good life in the good society. Rousseau reminds us of the natural man and the belief that man has potentialities which can be developed if only artificial restraints and prejudices can be overcome. So it is with Whitehead. Beyond his special insights and recommendations about the course of study, there stands the central idea that since the various sciences and fields of study are the result of isolation and abstraction, genuine education can be accomplished only if we can show how all the abstractions are interconnected to reflect the fundamental unity of life and direct experience. Knowledge comes by parts; education and understanding have to do with wholes.

One might conclude from Whitehead's critique that he resolutely opposed all forms of specialization in favor of some program of total general education. Such a conclusion would be false. He urged the need for specialized, concentrated study, but he did not regard it as an end in itself. He acknowledged the fact that mastery of a special field of study represents the highest fulfillment of the understanding, but he refused to ignore the perils of specialization. The point is of peculiar importance for the American scene. That we have been most successful in developing specialized study is clear from the high quality of our graduate and professional schools, but we have not always understood the perils and promises of that specialization. Too often it has happened that the lower school has been made to bear the entire responsibility for "general" education and cultural development, as if these preliminaries to specialist study could be acquired once for all and then pushed into the background in order to make room for graduate study

in the student's chosen field of interest or ability. This division
is ruinous and detrimental. General education becomes diffused and undisciplined and special study becomes narrow,
too self-conscious, and lacking in relevance to present life.
Whitehead's comment on this situation is instructive:

> . . . there is not one course of study which merely gives
> general culture, and another which gives special knowl-
> edge. The subjects pursued for the sake of a general
> education are special subjects specially studied; and, on
> the other hand, one of the ways of encouraging general
> mental activity is to foster a special devotion. (*The
> Aims of Education*, 23, Mentor edition.)

Of particular importance for our situation is the suggestion of
more creative possibilities within specialized study. It was
Whitehead's contention that devoted study of a particular field
is the only way in which the virtues of precision, the sense of
relevance, and economy of thought can be achieved. This
means that we must not look upon progress in education as a
move merely from the general to the special. The truth is that
both aspects go together and interpenetrate. The aim is to
bring together in one mind both skill in the analysis of details
and subtlety in the handling of abstract or general ideas. The
two go hand in hand; they can be kept together only if there
is some form of concentrated study at every level. Whitehead's
point is that specialized study, properly conducted, can lead
to general comprehension and not just to detailed knowledge
of a narrow range of things. General education, on the other
hand, loses its value in leading to comprehensive understanding unless the subjects studied are pursued in a rigorous and
intensive way.

Education in America has profited and can continue to profit
from the application of Whitehead's ideas. Much that he wrote

about learning and the schools betrays a deep interest in, and appreciation for, the educational venture in America. He was aware, as many Americans are not, of the permanent influence on American life exercised by our Puritan forbears, with their great passion for founding schools and advancing learning.

Two features of American educational practice especially engaged Whitehead's attention and won his admiration. He applauded our interest in experimentation, our willingness to open up new paths and run the risks of putting novel schemes into operation. He was no less appreciative of the belief, deeply rooted in the American past, that education is not an ornament "for its own sake" but is rather dedicated to the service of life and the enhancement of civilization. In an address delivered at the foundation of the Harvard Business School, Whitehead expressed sincere approval of the new venture, pointing out that America was taking the lead in developing forms of training adapted to the demands of a changing and growing society. With the growth of business as a specialized vocation, there arose the need for technical and concentrated study of the complex structure of the market place and the financial system which sustains it. The great universities of the past found their power in successfully meeting the demands made upon them by the societies in which they flourished. These universities became identified with the aim of training men in medicine, the law, or for service in the church. The development of American education is no exception. If business plays a major role, then any university which addresses itself to the concerns of the society about it cannot afford to ignore it. The inclusion of a school of business within the confines of a large university may have seemed to many to be a strange and "unacademic" development; Whitehead refused to follow that traditionalist view. Instead he saw in the foundation of such a school another illustration of American openness to new ideas and the responsiveness of the American university to the society in which it lives.

Whitehead's doubts about some features of America's pragmatic philosophy have already been pointed out. His refusal, however, to accept a thorough-going instrumentalist theory of mind and knowledge did not in the least diminish his belief that education must be controlled by purposes and that, in the end, everything we know meets its ultimate test in the actual living. To sustain and enhance life; these are the goals of all thought and knowledge. Whitehead, though himself a product of a different educational system, joined in supporting the characteristically American belief that the products of man's intellect must not be allowed to remain as recondite adjuncts to life, or as mere monuments to creative genius.

VI

RETROSPECT AND PROSPECT

The "golden period of American philosophy," as it has been called, the period of James, Royce, and Peirce, extends from just after the Civil War to the nineteen-thirties. It falls between what is generally known as the "classic background" of American thought — the age reaching back to Jonathan Edwards and Samuel Johnson of King's College — and the developments of the present. The golden period marks the coming of age of philosophical thinking in America and it embraces our best-known philosophical minds. They shaped and brought to clearest expression what we have called the "spirit of American philosophy." Can we now summarize that spirit as a prelude to asking about its presence on the current scene?

The answer to this question must begin with a word about the idea of "spirit" itself. By the spirit of a philosophical development is meant something which is at once more and less than a set of doctrines. A spirit is something more because it means, in addition to formulated beliefs, a style, a stance toward life in the world, and strong convictions about the importance of reflective thought. A spirit is something less than a body of consciously formulated doctrines because it stands deeply rooted in the life of a people as a kind of unwritten philosophy. In the figure used by Peirce, it would be in our muscles prior to finding its way into our learned tradition. Un-

187

fortunately, the annoying fact about styles and unwritten philosophies is that, while we may apprehend them in some not very clear way by living in the society animated by them, we are unable to communicate them to others unless we express them in the form of definite beliefs or doctrines. This we must do, but accompanied by the hope that what has been said about the peculiar character of a "spirit" will not be forgotten.

There are three dominant or focal beliefs through which our philosophic spirit can be articulated. First, the belief that thinking is primarily an *activity* in response to a concrete situation and that this activity is aimed at solving problems. Second, the belief that ideas and theories must have a "cutting edge" or must *make a difference* in the conduct of people who hold them and in the situations in which they live. Third, the belief that *the earth can be civilized* and obstacles to progress overcome by the application of knowledge. Taken together, these beliefs define a basically humanistic outlook — in the end, the spirit of philosophical thinking in America represents another outcropping of that ancient tradition established by the reflective genius of Socrates and Plato in which the Good is the dominant category. From this perspective all things derive their value from the contribution they make to the founding and securing of the good life.

These three beliefs are equally basic, although the philosophers whose views we have considered do not illustrate them in the same manner or to the same degree. When it is said that thought is an activity and a response to a situation, several distinct but related ideas are involved. For the pure rationalist fond of emphasizing the timeless character of conceptual meanings and of logical connections, it appears beside the point to describe thought in terms of the concrete setting in which it takes place. For the rationalist, to emphasize the fact that thinking is an activity, that it takes time, and that it is carried on by individual human beings, means no more than to call attention to a "psychological" aspect which really does not enter into the essential nature of thought. Not so for Peirce, James, Royce, and Dewey. Each in his own way started with the insight that thought — better, thinking — is an activity which is engaged in by human beings and that it emerges in human life under specific conditions. In other words, what Dewey called the *context* of thought, the historical setting and its problems, enters essentially into the meaning of reflective activity. Thinking is not something which happens in a world apart from or beyond the one in which all live; on the contrary, it is called forth by circumstances in our own world and it is responsive both to the demands imposed by the environment and to the interests of the individual thinker.

Of special importance is the reciprocal relation that exists between demand and response. The doctrine that reflective thinking is and must be oriented toward specific problems is the counterpart of the thesis that such thinking is called forth only upon occasions when there is some incongruity or lack of adjustment between the thinking individual and the concrete situation confronting him. The theory underlying this description expresses a teleological process not always acknowledged. It tells us that since reflective thinking arises only when the smooth operation of habit is interrupted by a problem, the whole function of such thinking must be to solve that problem. Thinking becomes a means to an end; its purpose is solving problems. This theory has been the occasion for sharp differences of opinion among the thinkers we have considered.

While each of them accepted the general thesis that thinking is directed by purposes and oriented toward the good, Peirce, Royce, and Whitehead differed sharply from James and Dewey on the issue of thought's autonomy. The first three argued for the universal character of thought and for its independence of *individual* plans and purposes. It is interesting to notice that, in contrast with James and Dewey, they were all proponents of *formal* logic and their interest in this subject and in the related mathematical fields led them to reject any theory which puts thought wholly under the constraint of extra-rational factors or purely practical considerations.

The difference of outlook is by no means unimportant. James and Dewey, though divided in their views at several crucial points, were at one in rejecting the ancient rationalist ideal according to which reason has its own goal and canons of truth. Pragmatism meant in the end the subordination of rational thought to an immanent, human, and practical goal; for the pragmatists the criterion of reason stands outside of reason in the sense that it is found in the success or failure of thinking to reach a desired practical goal. While Royce was willing to speak of logic as the expression of rational purpose; while Peirce was ready to say that thought has the function of producing belief and shaping habit; and while Whitehead could speak of the practical reason which Ulysses shares with the foxes; *no one of them was willing to make the test of reason consist in wholly non-cognitive terms.* Instead each maintained the ancient ideal of rational truth. Royce spoke of the rational will to know the whole truth as known to the Absolute Self. Peirce envisaged a community of knowers seeking a truth independent of the interests of any one member. Whitehead laid down criteria for judging the validity of a speculative scheme which presuppose that reason can exercise a distinctively intellectual function. The doctrine, therefore, that thinking is an activity performed by man, that it is a means of answering questions and of resolving problems, is broader than pragmatism itself. The latter position is one form only of the general thesis. Characterized by the special claim that since reflective thinking arises only when the situation presents a challenge or a difficulty, it finds its final test in its ability to achieve a practical goal. Not all of our philosophers would accept that claim.

To understand the spirit of American philosophy it is necessary to take full account of the distinction just developed. While thinkers like Peirce, Royce, and Whitehead had their own interpretation of thought as an activity carried on by individual persons in an historical setting, they did not accept the pragmatist thesis that the practical context of thought sets all the conditions for judging the validity of the ideas and theories which result from rational activity. This does not mean that in rejecting pragmatism as a philosophical doctrine they wanted to return to an older rationalism in which the concrete setting of thought does not count. On the contrary, they believed that reason can intervene in human life, that it can establish connections with human purposes and goals without at the same time losing its autonomy. It is an error to ignore, as critics sometimes have, the fact that many American thinkers who have talked about the function of reason in human life or the intimate connection between logic and the human will have at the same time refused to accept a place in the ranks of the pragmatists.

The second feature of the philosophic spirit in America — the belief that ideas must have a "cutting edge," that they must make a difference in human life and conduct — has long been regarded as the essence of the American character. Two basic ideas are involved: one is that thinking should be focused not on the universal, general, and "timeless" problems, but rather on specific difficulties arising here and now; the second is that the power of ideas to shape the course of events depends directly on the extent to which they are acted upon and used to guide the conduct of men.

By specific problems are meant such questions as, how to

improve *this* school system; how to resolve *this* conflict between labor and management; how to tame *this* river and turn it into a source of power. Such questions came to be regarded as the proper targets of thought because of the feeling that, since they have a "here and now" about them, their solutions can readily be used to transform a situation or guide our conduct. The contention has been that our total intellectual energy should be aimed at meeting these issues and that we have no time for dealing with problems of a generalized nature which have no clear focal point in time. Dewey expressed this point very well when he said that all our efforts should be aimed at eliminating the *evils* of human life, but that we have no time to speculate about the *problem of evil*. The complaint is that the latter is a metaphysical and religious question and the answer to it does not show us *how* to do away with poverty, disease, and injustice in particular situations.

Closely connected with this focus on specific problems is the belief that intellectual activity is justified to the extent to which its results are translated into action. Ideas that make a difference are those upon which people act. An idea must not merely inform us or please us, but rather it must move us to action and to the changing of our ways. If an idea does neither, it is worthless and may be ignored. The "practical" orientation so often associated with American life and thought is most evident at this point; an idea is a "mere" idea unless we can see how a situation is changed through the medium of that idea. If, after having the idea, everything remains the same as it was before, then the idea makes no difference — it is without a cutting edge.

The demand that thought be directed to specific problems expresses not only the American concern for locating and overcoming immediate difficulties; it expresses as well some embarrassment in the face of speculative questions about the foundations of life and the meaning of death. If the demand reveals a high confidence in the power of thought to resolve immediate problems, it also betrays a tendency to underestimate man's nature as a reflective animal. It is not a matter of the traditional clash between theory and practice, but rather of the difference between distinct types of questions. In a complex, technological culture we encounter immediate problems stemming from a multitude of maladjustments and failures in the spheres of business, politics, economic development, education, and public health. The specific and immediate problems are largely of a "practical" sort in the sense that their solution calls for technical knowledge and the proposal of definite courses of action.

Unhappily confusion sets in at the point where "real" problems are identified with those immediate difficulties which the instrumental intelligence can handle. The fundamental question is whether the "problems of men" are all of this kind. May it not be that there are times when the most "practical" problems of all, the problems whose solutions will make the greatest difference both to individuals and the society at large, are the largely speculative questions of the kind called "useless" by the practically oriented reason? This possibility has been a constant source of uneasiness for the American mind. Even if we define man as the tool-making and problem-solving animal, the question still remains as to *which* problems he will tackle. The fact is that man is more than a technician; he is a reflective being who is concerned about himself, his nature and destiny. Not all of the problems he confronts are of the sort which the pragmatic intelligence finds congenial. James and Royce saw this most clearly, despite the divergence in their views on other topics. Each saw that man is a being for whom such questions as the meaning of responsibility, the reality of God, the place of intelligent beings in the universe, and the status of beauty, are all "practical" problems of the highest importance. And yet they are precisely of the sort which Dewey, for example, advised us to disregard. These issues differ from the sort of immediate, specific problem generally called "real" by the typical hard-headed American. They differ in their scope especially, because they refer to life and the world as a whole rather than to some special province. They may have their special import for this or that person, but they are general in character, referring to man as man and to the relatively permanent nature of things. Nevertheless they cannot be ignored nor can they be spirited away as "impractical." Since mid-century it has become increasingly clear that questions about man and his inner life — his morality, his religion, his sanity — have taken command as the "real" problems of men.

The primacy of action remains, nevertheless. Ever since the days of Jonathan Edwards action has been taken as the chief clue to the sincerity of the individual. Willingness to act upon a belief, especially one involving risk, meant that a person took seriously what he professed to believe. This often meant that the active part of man's nature overshadowed the purely intellectual, the aesthetic, and the religious. Here William James set the pattern. Ideas and beliefs reveal their true meaning when we know the conduct to which they lead. Gradually there was established the idea that thought must be limited to what has direct bearing on human conduct; the notions that cannot be translated into some course of action were to be ignored.

Whatever belongs to religious interpretation, aesthetic appreciation, and the satisfaction of speculative curiosity is finally overshadowed by overt activity aimed at control of the external environment. When James, for example, interpreted religion and theology he found it difficult to attach meaning to such theological concepts as guilt and atonement because he could not see how they might be translated into human conduct. Despite his deep understanding of religion as a living force in life, and his sympathetic description of its many forms, he did not take seriously enough man's quest for *understanding*, his need for a unified outlook on the world which takes us beyond action and striving. Job, for example, passionately hoped for the end of his troubles and sufferings, but he sought even more fervently for an understanding of the world, for a ground of belief in the basic justice of things; he sought for an answer to the question: Why do human beings suffer? The answer to that question, if indeed an answer can be found, will not dictate a course of action; it will not tell us what to do if we want to eliminate suffering, although such an answer may well help us to face the world and its terrors with courage and resolve.

The third belief defining the American philosophic spirit strikes the note of optimism for which America has both been praised and attacked from within and without. The belief says that the environment of life can be transformed in accordance with human desires, that the face of nature can be civilized, and that major obstacles to progress can be overcome by the application of knowledge. This belief is the clearest expression of the American will; it represents what Santayana called "aggressive enterprise" and the spirit that inhabits the American skyscraper. Dewey gave to this belief its most forceful utterance. It coincides with his instrumental view of intelligence. Underneath it all is the conviction that no problems exist which are, in principle, incapable of being solved through applied knowledge. The universe presents no ultimate riddles and it sets no absolute limits to human ingenuity and skill. Wherever problems are encountered or obstacles arise, there is the place for human intelligence to demonstrate its ability to meet and master external circumstances.

Until recent years, this optimistic creed was directed largely to the external environment. The knowledge gained by the natural sciences was supposed to provide the means for meeting the obstacles to human development posed by physical nature. The knowledge and insight of the social sciences and of philosophy were to arm us against the problems arising out of historical and social life. The emphasis was objective and external in the sense that little attention was paid to the problem of subjective or internal controls. Man is the one who brings knowledge to bear upon the course of events and he is sovereign over the empire of intelligence. That man himself might prove to be the greatest problem and obstacle to progress was not, until recently, considered as a serious possibility. It is curious in the extreme that, apart from the researches of James, the problems of the human self, exposed by the work of Freud, were not taken seriously. It is not that important contributions had not been made by those working within the rapidly growing science of psychology; it is rather that throughout the years we have described as the golden period of American thought, little attention was paid to the concerns and problems most closely connected with the individual person. The tendency was to consider man as one more animal besides others, albeit more complex. If man was acknowledged to have a problematic side, the difficulty was usually minimized by saying that he only lacked knowledge or was insufficiently dedicated to the aims of science. The possibility that the ego has depths not to be apprehended by the experimental method or mastered by the instrumental intelligence was quietly passed by. Instead attention was directed to the attack upon the environment; it was believed that nature and history present the most troublesome stumbling blocks to progress and that it is they that must be conquered. The many crises which have characterized American life at mid-century have been due to an awareness that this old creed is inadequate. It is becoming clearer that controlling the external world is not enough and that more attention must be paid to the distinctively human problems of morality, of religion, and of art.

To sum up the spirit of philosophical thinking in America as it existed until mid-century, we may say that it represented a modern version of the ancient humanistic tradition which runs from ancient Greece through the Renaissance and the Enlightenment to the present day. American thinkers have been primarily "moralists" in the sense that, howsoever strong their interest in nature and in science has been, their ultimate focus has been on the uses of knowledge and the values of things for human purposes. The instrumental has been judged superior to the intrinsic and more often than not usefulness has been taken as its own final justification.

So much for the retrospect; the golden period of American philosophy is over and has been gone for some time. Where are we now and what of the future? The spirit which made itself evident in the works of the classical American thinkers is not dead, but profound changes have taken place since the days when pragmatism was dominant. These changes have by no means been confined to the internal development of ideas. The world has passed through a second war of global proportions, the atomic age is upon us with all of its implications both for war and for peace, the international political situation has turned into a two-sided ideological struggle, and America has been thrust into the center of world politics to deal with problems new and strange to a relatively young country endowed with so much power. One of the results of these developments is a new interest in goals and purposes and a more acute awareness of the limitations of the merely instrumental intelligence. Upheavals abroad and insecurities at home have served to bring into clearer focus questions about genuine values and worthwhile aims. Americans are not as sure as they once were that if questions of means can be solved, the ends will take care of themselves.

What has happened to philosophical thinking in the midst of the new situation? Anyone who is acquainted with recent developments is bound to be puzzled by the turn of events. Pragmatism, which embodied so much of the American philosophic spirit, was an indigenous philosophical movement. Even so vigorous a critic as Royce acknowledged that fact and our study of James, Peirce, and Dewey has served to underscore the point. Pragmatism grew out of American life and experience; it was not in the main an academic movement, and its chief expositors were men marked by independence of judgment. Although they were aware of past traditions in philosophy, there was no tendency whatever on the part of Peirce, James, Royce, and Dewey to imitate others or to adopt fashions of thought to gain the approval of thinkers in any other part of the world. Despite his own adverse judgment upon much that pragmatism stood for, Santayana had to admit that the type of thinking it represented was honest and genuinely expressive of American life. The puzzling fact is that pragmatism as a comprehensive outlook on things could not sustain itself, at least among academic philosophers. The fact that journalists and politicians continue to speak of "America's pragmatic philosophy" is to be explained by what the social scientists used to call the "cultural lag." The truth is that as we moved into the decade of the 'forties other influences were at work and they exerted pressure in new directions.

The revival of British empiricism through the writings of Bertrand Russell, G. E. Moore, and subsequent analytic philosophers meant a return of the conception of experience against which the pragmatists had fought. It meant a return to experience as "sense data" and to skepticism about the role of reason in human affairs. Moreover, the powerful invasion of Continental positivism with its emphasis on logic, language, and the analysis of natural science fostered this return to the older empiricism. Positivism also helped bring about a reorientation in philosophical thinking. Gone was interest in the "problems of men"; gone was the sense that philosophical thinking is relevant to the most concrete human interests and concerns. Instead the older questions about the theory of knowledge were revived and the task of philosophy was limited to investigating the language and logic of science. Practical or immediate issues were set aside and speculative problems dismissed. A positive spirit came to prevail; the aim was to disclose and remain within the confines of the brute or bare fact. The piling of fact upon fact and the belief that somehow facts arrange and synthesize themselves came to replace the quest for rational explanations.

It cannot, however, be overlooked that there was a certain emphasis in Dewey's thought particularly which gave rise to the idea that all inquiry must fall within the scope of the special sciences. I refer to his frequent criticism of "wholesale" questions, for example, his claim that there is no problem of the relation between thought and things *überhaupt*, and his consequent stress on "retail" or specific questions. To many it seemed that if the genuine problems are all of a specific sort which arise when habit fails or custom falters, then such problems can be dealt with by the specialized knowledge of the sciences. Philosophical interpretation seemed superfluous. Since the pragmatists had paid considerable attention to problems of social organization, politics, education and economic welfare, it was a short step to the conclusion that the social sciences might well be the effective heirs of philosophy. What need is there, it was asked, for a reflective inquiry over and above the instrumental thinking required for resolving the problems which arise in society? The answer often given was, no need at all.

If the practical questions which the pragmatists had taken as the essence of philosophy were translated into the social or "policy" sciences as they came to be called, logical empiricism was aiming from another side at the elimination of speculative questions by reducing philosophy to a purely critical instrument. According to the logical empiricist program, philosophy is essentially a matter of disclosing the logical structure of science by attending to the language in which scientific conclusions are couched. Later forms of analytic philosophy followed the pattern of regarding philosophy as the analysis of language, but they differed from the older logical empiricism or positivism in refusing to limit themselves to the language of natural science and logic. Largely through the influence of Ludwig Wittgenstein, analytic philosophy extended itself to include various uses of language, ranging from so-called "ordinary" language at one end of the spectrum to the language of religion and philosophy at the other. Common to all forms of analytic philosophy has been the belief that philosophy has nothing of its own to add to our stock of knowledge; it is instead a technique for talking about the logic and the grammar of the language used by others.

Regardless of the explanations, the fact remains that professional philosophers in America for the most part turned away from classical pragmatism and sought instead to assimilate the approach and the ideas of British analytic philosophy and the doctrines of Continental thought. Whatever its shortcomings, however, pragmatism represented a genuine belief in philosophy as an independent discipline and it kept alive, albeit in modern dress, some of the perennial problems with which philosophers have always occupied themselves. The consequences for philosophy in America stemming from this shift in attention have been considerable.

The first consequence is complex. On the one hand is the loss of the audience, and on the other, the passing, especially in the universities, of the philosophical problems neglected by professional philosophers into the hands of people who lack the special training required for dealing with them. In the days of James and Royce, people of diverse interests and in various walks of life read philosophical books and concerned themselves with philosophical issues. Philosophy was not considered a topic existing in a world apart; it belonged instead to the range of subjects to be taken seriously by every thinking person. Recently the picture has changed radically. Exclusive concentration on technical problems of logic, of semantics, and of the theory of knowledge has made it all but impossible for those outside the ranks of professional philosophy to read philosophical books with profit. The development, moreover, of an academic approach marked by a technical vocabulary and the habit of casting problems in a form known only to professional philosophers who have kept up with the periodical literature adds to the difficulties. Not only are the problems treated far removed from living experience, but the manner in which they are stated and discussed is often designed to lead to the traditional empiricist answers. A genuine dialogue between different positions is missing.

Philosophical issues, like other serious questions, do not disappear merely because they are ignored. If they are not raised explicitly by those who are supposed to treat them, they have a habit of obtruding themselves where they are least expected. In many universities throughout the country at present, those working in literature, history, depth psychology, and, in some cases, even the natural sciences, are more involved with the larger philosophical questions than the official philosophers themselves. Literary critics tackle the question of the nature of art and its relation to religion and morality; intellectual historians concern themselves with the interconnections between the different fields of study and with the impact of ideas upon culture; depth psychologists puzzle over the meaning of human freedom and the nature of responsibility; physicists argue about the issues of determinism and mechanism; and life scientists ask about the correct interpretation of purposive behavior. The situation is even more striking in the fields of medicine and the law. Doctors, reflecting on the excesses of specialization in medical research, have stimulated interest in the need for treating the total personality, and lawyers have never been more concerned over the problems of jurisprudence and questions centering on the status and authority of the law. In too many cases, philosophers have followed in the wake of these developments instead of having been a moving force in launching them.

Unhappily, training is required for dealing with philosophical questions and those who raise them inadvertently or as a side line in connection with their principal field of study are not likely to have the necessary training. The result is that we are offered a variety of well-meant but ill-considered "outlooks," "reflections," and "world views" written by men for whom a philosophical scheme is no more than a tissue of personal reflections and insights. These efforts generally lack clarity and, especially, proper respect for the subtlety of philosophical inquiry. The critical tests of comprehensiveness and internal coherence are ignored; discipline is lost. The situation is deplorable and yet it is inevitable when professional philosophy becomes identified with technical questions considered apart from the concrete experience and life from which they arise. In the end we suffer from a great divorce; on the one hand stands technical philosophy pursued with great skill and much rigor but with results that are largely devoid of content applicable to current life. On the other stand various forms of informal philosophy which, though frequently aimed at the important questions, are without discipline and focus. A major task of the future is to find creative ways of bridging the gap, of bringing rigorous philosophy back to the larger questions and of extending philosophical training so that more of those working in special fields of inquiry will be alive to the importance of philosophical questions and will be better equipped to deal with them.

The second and by far more puzzling development on the philosophical scene in America is a loss of independence in thinking. At several points we have spoken of the originality and independence of the classical American thinkers. They thought for themselves about problems arising directly from American life and experience; they had no tendency whatever to follow academic patterns or to shape their thoughts in order to meet rules set up by others. For a variety of reasons not at all easy to fathom, professional philosophers in America have changed the situation profoundly during the past twenty years. Many have been too willing to imitate techniques and adopt doctrines set forth by others without considering their relevance to the culture in which they live. Philosophy in America has fallen under the domination of British thought to an extent unequaled since the eighteenth century. Embarrassed by the looseness of much philosophical discussion carried on under the banner of pragmatism and anxious to prove that philosophy is scientific in character, many younger thinkers have gravitated toward British analytical thinking. The attractions are its clarity and the feeling of mastery which comes from exercising control over the major instrument of communication —language. Moreover, the hard-headed empiricism characteristic of the British tradition has seemed to bring philosophy back to earth after the dialectical subtleties of American rationalism and idealism. Insofar as analytic philosophy attends to natural language and the meaning of words in actual use it embraces a genuine empirical element that is lacking in the thought of those who concentrate exclusively on formal or artificial languages.

There can be no doubt that language furnishes the key to the current situation. It is obvious, despite all the bad jests made about the difference between American English and British English, that the existence of a common language makes possible a philosophical exchange which cannot be carried out with the same intensity between American philosophers and those in any other part of the world. Even in an age of translations, works in English are more readily available than those in any other language. Loss of independence has come about because on the whole American thinkers, not bound as tightly by a rigid and homogeneous academic tradition, have paid more attention to British thought than British philosophers have to American thinking. But this is not the only sense in which language has played a crucial role in the process. The belief that philosophy begins and ends with the study of language has the effect of directing attention exclusively to what has *already been* expressed or articulated. The analysis of language, at least as carried on within the schools of linguistic philosophy, results in the disclosure of *past* thought and experience. The linguistic approach to philosophy, whatever its merits may be, is a conservative enterprise. It leads to the neglect of *present* life and experience. In hoping to find the meaning of what has already found expression in language, the linguistic analyst is apt to ignore the fresh, flowing, and novel experience in the midst of which he lives. Failure to confront current experience means loss of independence in thinking; it means bondage to what others have already said. The belief that philosophical questions can be answered merely by attending to what has already been said or to what people "really mean" when they say what they do, is too simple. First, the belief is based on the mistaken assumption that everything of importance has already been expressed, and secondly, language becomes a barrier betweeen the thinker and the actual situation in which he exists. When that happens, he is tempted to attend to the language and ignore the situation. Just as in the old empiricism where sense data came as a kind of screen between the thinker and the object before him, so language takes its place as the medium which often cuts the philosopher off from the novel experience unfolding all around him. The recovery of independence in thinking takes place when the thinker makes his own attempt to reflect on the meaning of personality, society, history, or God, setting out from his own experience. To begin and end by asking what these words mean, or by hoping to discover the answer in the writings of other philosophers, is to remain in bondage to the past.

Having reached the ninth decade of this century we have a new vantage point from which to survey the philosophical developments that have taken place on the American scene over the past fifty years. One can see even more clearly than was possible twenty years ago what consequences stemmed from the failure to sustain not so much the doctrines of our classical philosophers as their concern for the philosophical problems that arise out of the broad spectrum of American culture. Such questions are as obvious as they are urgent. What is to be done about the erosion of religious concern? How is it possible to maintain individual responsibility and personal integrity in a society dominated by huge corporations? What basis can there be for freedom and moral values in a technological society largely concerned with things? These and countless other problems posed by advances in science, new possibilities in genetic engineering, ecological imbalances, not to mention the ethical dilemmas confronting us as individuals and representatives of professions are basically reflective or philosophical concerns. It

is my contention that the sort of concrete philosophical thinking manifested by those whose thought has been presented in
the preceding chapters of this book was interrupted by the
growth of a purely academic type of philosophy concerned
more with tools and techniques than with basic ethical, political, metaphysical, and religious questions. That interruption,
moreover, was marked by the deepest irony, for while the
pragmatists had been vigorously questioning the main assumptions of classical empiricism, and especially the need to *begin*
with epistemology, the philosophies of analysis and of positivism then imported continued to maintain those assumptions as
if they had never been challenged. If any attention was paid to
the thought of Peirce, James, and Dewey it was often merely
for the purpose of showing that Pragmatism paved the way for
the reception of the new analytic philosophies.

In support of my contention, I shall set forth five main points
of criticism concerning philosophy during the time when it has
been dominated by analysis and the linguistic turn.

I

First, and most fundamental, is serious questioning of the
validity of the *reflexive turn* and of the linguistic turn insofar
as it continues the idea that all philosophical discussion must
be *preceded* by some form of preliminary analysis—logical,
epistemological, linguistic—supposed necessary for clearing
the ground and putting our intellectual tools in proper order.
There are at least three grounds on which to call into question
the validity and even the possibility of this approach. Much of
the epistemology supposed to be a necessary propadeutic to
philosophy has been based on some form of the doctrine that
we know *intuitively* that the object of "immediate awareness" is

internal to the mind and distinct from the so-called external
world. But, as Peirce showed in his articles of the 1860's, all
thinking takes place within the medium of signs and no one can
be said to know intuitively the logical status of any content
known, i.e., that it is present *only* to the mind of the knower.
One can *argue* that the immediate awareness is something internal on the basis of the relativity of perception or in order
to maintain certainty by reducing the extent of the cognitive
claim, but one is not entitled to the conclusion upon which all
the arguments as to how we are to reach the external world by
starting on the "inside" have been based as an intuitive deliv-
erance. The point is that if there is no certainty in knowing
that we start on the "inside" these epistemological problems
vanish and we are free to start thinking from where we actually are, namely beings who have inherited a stock of commonsense beliefs about an objective world which are called into
question only when new facts collide with them and call for a
readjustment. If, however, we are required to prove that we
are not encapsulated in "experience" and have reached the
"external world" in advance of any inquiry into specific questions and subject matters, all further intellectual endeavor,
scientific as well as philosophical, would have to be suspended.
In fact, an examination of the assumptions of the problem
makes it clear that, stated in those terms, the problem is insoluble. Consider that we are to begin not only with some immediate data of sense, but also with the supposed certainty
that these data are confined to the knowing mind and the task
is to find a warrant for supporting the claim that the external
world has been reached. That the problem is insoluble in these
terms can readily be seen from the fact that the only allowable
evidence on which one could argue would be the same sort of
"internal" data that bring about the problem of the external
world in the first place. Increase the density of internal data

as much as you will, its status does not change. There is no magical transition to objectivity starting with those assumptions, and, in fact, no possible transition at all.

II

A second objection to the need for epistemological preliminaries stems from calling into question what has come to be called "foundationalism" or the thesis that all knowledge must *begin* with some privileged items—clear and distinct ideas, the first impressions of sense, intuitively certain axioms, etc.— said to be certain and needed to form the basis of the body of knowledge built upon them. Apart from the well-known fact that many of these "certainties" have later turned out to be false or only partially true, there is the irony that philosophers continued the "quest for certainty" even in the face of the fact that the sciences, taken by many of these same philosophers as the paradigm of knowledge, had accepted fallibilism and recognized the inescapability of the need for a provisional component limiting conclusions to the actual weight of the evidence. It was one of the merits of the pragmatists to detect this irony and propose that philosophy should accept the same fallibilism while also rejecting the questionable demand of the skeptic that either one has (or claims) certainty or one has no knowledge at all.

III

A third argument against the primacy of critical philosophy is directed not against the need for a controlled or critical procedure in every reflective enterprise, but rather against a

merely formal analysis of our knowing apparatus totally divorced from a consideration of that apparatus at work. The
test of the adequacy, fruitfulness, comprehensiveness, and
coherence of any set of categories, leading principles, and hypotheses is not found in an examination of them when they are
"idling" in our understanding, but rather when they are at
work in the actual process of describing, interpreting, and explaining what we encounter. The pragmatists, in my view,
were right in shifting the focus of attention from the issues of
traditional epistemology to matters of methodology, not primarily for the reason Dewey gave, namely that the former
deals only with knowledge *überhaupt* while the latter concerns
specific issues, because methodology is also a generic affair.
The point is rather that a theory of knowledge taken by itself
is insufficient for determining the validity of any particular
answer to a given question in a special field of empirical inquiry. To assess the truth/falsity, adequacy/inadequacy of a
scientific hypothesis or a philosophical theory requires that we
determine the extent to which it actually explains, illuminates,
interprets the range of items it covers. In short, our knowing
apparatus must be "in gear" and engaged in some actual intellectual enterprise in order for us to determine its degree of
success in resolving the problem or question that first set it in
motion. And, I should add, we are here talking not about "success" in the sense of some individual or group advancing its
own interests in the world, but of *intellectual* success whether
philosophical or scientific, i.e., the adequacy of a hypothesis to
the evidence, or of an answer to a question. To proceed in any
other way simply leads to the postponement of actual questions
and problems, because, instead of moving ahead with a proposal to be assessed, the discussion is allowed to lapse into a
world of subjunctives, how we *would* go about dealing with the
issue, the language we *would* use, the logic we *would* adopt,

etc., except that the preliminary analysis exhausts everyone
and the first-order question disappears or goes unanswered.
No better illustration of this point could be found than the
entire development of "meta-ethics." Until quite recently when
pressing issues of human rights, the status of women, problems
in biomedical ethics,and others have led philosophers back to
substantive questions, the age-long discussion of the nature of
the good life, what responsibilities we have, issues of personal
and public morality were all *postponed* because of the belief
that the philosopher's task is not to engage in "moralizing" but
to get the language and logic of ethics in order, presumably for
some future substantive use. Unfortunately, until there was
very great external pressure from beyond the confines of the
academy the substantive discussion was postponed by philosophers who continued to occupy themselves with problems at
the "meta" level, largely because of the belief that on that level
more "agreement" is possible.

A well-known form of the belief that agreement among philosophers can be achieved if some more "neutral" level or vantage point is occupied is to be found in Quine's notion of "semantic ascent," of a shift "from talk of objects to talk of words."
As Quine puts it, "The strategy of semantic ascent is that it
carries the discussion into a domain where *both parties are
better agreed* on the objects (*viz.*, words) and on the main
terms concerning them."* Two comments are in order concerning this strategy. First, the developments of the past two
decades in philosophy do not support the contention that there
is more agreement at the level of words than that of things, not
least because the nature, status, and function of words themselves represent issues on which there is disagreement. Secondly, even if there were more agreement at this linguistic

*W. Quine, *Word and Object* (Cambridge: MIT Press, 1960), pp. 271–72;
my italics.

level than there is, it would not follow that our understanding of things, of concrete experience, and of the situations out of which philosophical issues arise, had been enhanced.

The second point at which I would fault the analytic empiricism of the past forty years coincides with their continuation of the classical view of the nature of *experience*, despite the clear and pertinent criticism of that conception advanced not only by the pragmatists, but by such thinkers as Bergson, Whitehead, Heidegger, and the phenomenologists. Only Wittgenstein among linguistic philosophers came to appreciate the relevance of this criticism at the point where he began to consider the inadequacy of a single criterion of meaningfulness for discourse and paid attention to the variety in the *use* of language, something close to what the pragmatists meant when they spoke of differing *contexts*. It is difficult to do justice to the matter in a quite limited space, but at least four points are essential for an understanding of the need for a broader and more complex view of experience than that maintained in the tradition of modern empiricism. To begin with, experience as we know it by attending to actual experiencing cannot be identified with the contents of the senses and then set over against the conceptual, logical, linguistic, and grammatical components without which no experience is possible. As Kant pointed out— it is the central lesson of the *Critique*—nothing that can be called experience consists of sense content alone. But, more importantly, the genetic approach of classical empiricism resulted in identifying experience with its "first" or "simplest" elements, whether in the form of clearcut and atomic sense data or so-called protocol sentences, both of which are neither simple nor first because they represent the results of analysis or what Dewey called "reflected products." It is for this reason that no one, except perhaps a philosopher, ever "experiences" those brown patches or the instantaneous bit of the color red supposed to be expressed in protocol sentences. Actual experience has a field character with a temporal spread, involving a focal point or points and background or fringes. Consider even so elementary an experience as hearing a clap of thunder; that is not a bare datum of sound, but something that breaks in against a background of silence and thus comes as a contrasting surprise so that the full occasion of experience must be expressed as "startling-sound-breaking-silence-now-recollected-as-having-preceded-the-interrupting-focal-datum." Paradoxically, we become more vividly aware of the silence that was broken than we had been before. A second reason why experience became so truncated on the traditional view is that *contexts* were largely ignored and all the emphasis fell on the *content* taken in isolation, or if contexts were taken into account the dominant one was that of the theoretical knower or spectator passively registering the "given." But this is only one context of experience and if it is elevated to the status of a model or criterion for all experience, then the result can only be what has actually happened: the moral, esthetic, religious, existential, political contexts of experience will be excluded from any sort of *rational* treatment and forced into a domain of pure subjectivity.

Third, the classical view of experience was clearly biased in favor of disjunctions and separations with a corresponding neglect of connections, transitions, and tendencies. To take a simple example, the fact that the color of a book is *other than* its shape is no more privileged or basic as a bit of fact than that the pages are *with* each other and the cover. The togetherness and connections belong as fully to experience as the disjunctions and are not simply introduced by the mind. All experience, moreover, is shot through with relational signs that lead us from one part of it to another so that it is quite illegitimate to set thought, interpreting, and inferring over against "experience" as if some bare content alone belonged to the objectively real while the interpreting idea and word are taken as no more than "mental" additions.

Fourth, the classical view of experience made no attempt whatever to connect experiencing with habits and patterns of response answering to what we may call "knowing how" to execute some maneuvers or prepare an appropriate response to a situation. When we say of a doctor that he is "experienced" in dealing with cases of mental illness, of a lawyer that he is experienced in the conduct of criminal cases, or of an archaeologist that he is experienced in the handling of artifacts and interpreting their significance, we mean far more than that he has been in the *presence* of the relevant data or that he has been a passive recipient of what has been "given" to him. We mean instead to point to patterns of judgment and behavior developed over a period of time and involving many encounters with the material in question so that being "experienced" is a cumulative result, an art acquired through complex interactions between the subject and the situations he confronts. It is difficult to see how this important dimension of experience can be understood by any conception of experience that extends no further than individual occasions when sense contents have been encountered and recorded.

In addition to the critique of both the reflexive and linguistic turns for their postponement of first-order questions, and the exposure of the need for a more adequate account of actual experiencing than that derived from the tradition of Hume and Mill, there is a third consideration to be taken into account; some would say that it was the central concern of the pragmatists and certainly one that led to the sharpest response from their critics. I refer to their attempt to establish essential connections between thought and action, and between purpose and thought. I will not attempt to rehearse the long history of misunderstanding on these heads, and I do not deny that

James, especially, was responsible for much of it with his use of such terms as "success," "satisfaction," "cash value," and others that led critics like Russell to describe Pragmatism as "trans-Atlantic truth," implying that on this view thought is to be tested solely in terms of its capacity to lead to the sort of action that enables an individual to "succeed" in the world. The so-called futurism of Pragmatism is far more subtle and, above all, it does *not* mean that "all thought is for the sake of action." The emphasis on consequences and results is essentially an attempt to connect meaning with the conditional, dynamic manifestation of the characters of things whether in ordinary experience or under controlled laboratory conditions. I call this approach a "dynamizing" of the predicates; if an X is a Y, then we may expect that it *would* react, appear as, behave in such and such a way under certain conditions. In short, we move away from the traditional conception of things possessing qualities that we either sense or apprehend through the medium of clear and distinct ideas to situations in which such qualities actually manifest themselves in *interaction* with ourselves and other things. The reference to results and outcomes is primarily a way of emphasizing that actual testing is a process whereby we hope to discover whether an expected conditional mode of behavior is fulfilled or disappointed.

It is important to notice that the appeal to the behavior of things, what they would do in this or that situation, does not exhaust the role of action with respect to either meaning or truth. We must be concerned as well with the behavior of the subject when confronted with objects and situations calling for a response of some sort. Our knowledge of the conditional behavior of the things we encounter enables us to anticipate possible courses of action and to prepare the most appropriate response. To take a simple example, it belongs to the "meaning" of what it is to be a "bull" that anyone encountering the animal, knowing its pugnacious tendencies, will prepare for flight and a place of safety. Connecting the tendencies of the behavior of things with the *responses* we are to make to them is what Peirce had in mind when he spoke of ideas as "being in our muscles," orienting and directing our activity and not merely observing it as a spectator might do. The response of the subject is no less conditional than the behavior of the object. We say to ourselves, If X is a Y and the situation calls for me to respond to it, then I expect that I *would* do Z. None of this requires that we identify thought and action or reduce thought to behavior. Relating two items in an intelligible way does not imply that they are the same, and Peirce was vigorous in his denial that the meaning of a concept—"intellectual purport"— can ever be identical with any act since the latter is always determinate and singular while conceptual meaning is always general.

IV

My fourth reservation concerning the dominant trend in the philosophy of the past half century centers upon the linguistic turn. I am very far from wanting to say that the linguistic approach to philosophical issues has been without its own contribution. We have learned much, for example, about the different functions of language and especially the problems generated by the attempt to find a "basic" function to serve as a touchstone for all others. If, for instance, I am seeking to determine what is being communicated in a parabolic form of speech, I shall make a fundamental mistake if I ask for its "literal" meaning while ignoring the peculiarities of the parabolic mode. We have learned as well that the languages of large scale forms of experience—science, art, religion—are not homogeneous but that each contains within itself a multiplicity of different forms of expression requiring special attention in each case. In science, for example, there are observational statements, theoretical frameworks of greater or lesser scope, heuristic expressions serving as models and metaphors, predictive statements with probability components, etc., and while all these forms may be said to belong to the "language of science," each requires separate treatment in its own terms. Likewise in the language of religion we are confronted with devotional language that is quite different from theological language and with the languages of myth, exhortation, and narrative, all of which differ from both theological and devotional language.

The contributions made through the linguistic turn are not in question; my concern is rather with the limitations of that approach and the difficulty one encounters in bringing linguistic philosophers even to consider whether there are any limitations. The major problem is that of becoming encapsulated in a world of language. I do not mean the problem of a "private language," but rather that the concentration on language as an ultimate subject matter puts us in danger of losing contact with primary experience. The same sort of criticism advanced by James against a conceptual dialectic that is not continually related to the continuum of experience from which it was abstracted can be leveled against the linguistic approach. When our lowest level language is an "object" language, we are thereby confined to the realm of discourse and to what has already *been said*; it may be thought that an analysis of such expressions suffices without recourse to ongoing experience, to a return or a "second look" at the things and situations we are supposed to be talking about. But this is a mistake. If we knew by some oracular insight that everything has already been said and, further, that what has been said is perfectly adequately expressed, we might well dispense with the world altogether and busy ourselves with the clarification of our language. But since neither of these conditions obtains, we are forced to return to the extralinguistic situations and encounters in the world of experience where even philosophers must live. Too often, the contemporary student introduced to philosophy in the linguistic mode is led to consider issues primarily in terms of the meanings of words and their use. Some students think primarily of the *term* "freedom" and its meaning, for example, and not at all of the basic *experiences*—situations involving choice, deliberation, judgment, estimation of responsibilities— forming the matrix of the problem at hand. It is surely ironic to find philosophers who describe themselves as "empiricists" having so little respect for actual experience and walling themselves up in a world of *expression*. Experience, to be sure, is not accessible apart from expression, but it does not follow that the two are identical.

In view of these considerations, I find quite incredible the following statement made by Richard Rorty in *The Linguistic Turn*:

> Linguistic philosophy, over the past thirty years, has succeeded in putting the entire philosophical tradition, from Parmenides through Descartes and Hume to Bradley and Whitehead, on the defensive. . . . This achievement is sufficient to place this period among the great ages of the history of philosophy.*

What remains to be explained in this claim is precisely the merit that is supposed to attach itself to putting a philosophical tradition on the "defensive." The philosophers mentioned were all engaged in dealing with philosophical questions directly and candidly and, whatever view one may take of their positions,

*R. Rorty, *The Linguistic Turn* (Univ. of Chicago Press, 1967), p. 33

no one can deny that they were seriously concerned to bring to bear both philosophical insight and reflection on the dominant issues of their time. What is the result and the value of putting all these thinkers on the "defensive" especially when that means largely a sort of linguistic analysis of the way they formulated their problems aimed, not at dealing with these problems (or their contemporary counterparts), but rather at dissolving them as merely "philosophers'" problems that would never have arisen if more attention had been paid to "language." I fail to see what advance has been made in this development. Human beings do not cease to raise questions about the self, freedom, morality, and the like merely because some professional philosophers propose to show us that such questions arise as the result of the misuse of language. As subsequent experience shows, the questions remain but since philosophers try to avoid them, they pass into the hands of others who have no special aptitude for dealing with them. That is a curious sort of "progress" indeed.

A corollary of the foregoing is the basically conservative character of the linguistic approach concentrating, as it must, on the past tense in the form of what has already been uttered. Dewey made a similar point in connection with his critique of Locke and Hume and their emphasis on *data*, i.e., facts that are fully finished and done with, to the exclusion of what is yet to come. Neither in that empiricism nor in its linguistic counterpart can justice be done to what is in process or in the making, or what now needs to be said because it is novel and has not been expressed before. The pragmatists may have been over-sanguine in the stress they laid on the future as the mode of time over which we can hope to exercise some rational control, but they were alive to the growing edge of experience, its novelties and possibilities, and they would not allow their thought to become encapsulated in a past consisting entirely of finished fact.

V

Further reflection on the consequences of the linguistic turn carries us almost imperceptibly over into the fifth and last of the difficulties I find inherent in this approach. Stated briefly, the dominant mode of philosophical thinking in recent decades has led to an over-professionalization of the subject, and to the neglect, through loss of contact, of the larger and deep-seated problems of American culture. It was all but inevitable that philosophers, focusing entirely on language, would come to narrow that focus on the language of philosophers and to an increasing internalized discussion of what other philosophers have written. I am not unmindful of the approach through ordinary language which is certainly richer and reflective of a broader expanse of experience than the languages of science or logic. Nor do I want to minimize the contribution made in recent years by those who have explored the special "language games" characteristic of psychology, art, religion, politics, and other dimensions of experience. The difficulty is rather that so much of modern professional philosophy has been confined to the academy and discussion has revolved largely around philosophers' problems having to do with what I earlier on called the preliminaries, the setting of the logical and linguistic houses in order, and the postponement of the difficult issues of human life such as the preservation of responsibility in a mechanized society, the nature of the person and of personal freedom, the status of norms and ideals in a world dominated by fact, and countless others of equal importance. The best proof of the failure of philosophy at this point is the *migration* of many philosophical questions to other arenas, other disciplines because many professional philosophers have allowed them to go by default. Literary critics, intellectual historians, novelists, psychologists, speculatively oriented natural scientists, to say nothing of journalists, prize-fighters, joggers, and film stars, have all of late become "philosophers" in their discussion of questions with which philosophers used to deal before they became persuaded that they could not be dealt with until the tools and the ground were first made ready. I do not mean to suggest that philosophers "own" a special province, fenced off and posted with "No Trespassing" signs or that philosophical problems cannot be illuminated from many different perspectives. It is rather that many of those who have inherited what was once the concern of reflective thinkers do not have the training necessary for dealing in a clear and critical way with vague but important issues that are basically of great interest to large numbers of people. Many who do have this training are not dealing with those issues and that is why we have to endure what is so often no more than uncritical personal opinion on the part of amateur philosophers, or professionals in some other discipline turned amateur philosopher.

Not all philosophers in the past half-century have accepted the analytic or linguistic approach. Among those who have dissented and pursued other lines of thought are the followers of Whitehead and related forms of process philosophy, the philosophers of existence and some phenomenologists, the Heideggerians and the Marxists. The fact remains, however, that the mode of philosophy I have been criticizing has been the dominant position in American professional and academic philosophy, and that dominance was established and maintained in a quite peculiar way. Analytic philosophers have not, on the whole, thought of their position as merely one among others on a philosophical spectrum. Instead they have sought to *define* philosophy as a discipline to be carried on exclusively in the analytic mode; those who do not "do" philosophy, as the saying goes, in this way are declared not to be engaged in philosophy at all. I regard this claim as sheerly dogmatic and destructive in the end of any critical dialogue aimed at assessing the rela-

tive merits of different outlooks and points of view. To high-
light the corrosiveness of this dogmatic shift, consider some
comparisons drawn from the past. Aquinas and Ockham, for
example, differed most significantly in their views of the nature
of an individual, a difference that had important repercussions
for their positions with regard to other philosophical and theological issues. It is, however, quite inconceivable that either
thinker would have considered these differences grounds for
declaring that the other was not engaged in philosophical thinking. Locke obviously thought Descartes was wrong insofar as
he held the doctrine of innate ideas attacked at the beginning
of Locke's *Essay*, but there is no indication that Locke, on that
account, thought it necessary to exclude Descartes from the
province of philosophy. The same is true of the relation between Hume and Kant. The latter was quite sure that Hume
was mistaken in his analysis of causality, but there is no hint
that Kant wanted to deny that Hume was a truly philosophical
thinker.

Unfortunately, the modern situation is entirely different because the analytic philosophers have turned philosophy into a
technique and defined its borders in terms of that technique.
The chief result is loss of communication at the least and ex-
communication at the most if one refuses to make the assumptions and adopt the methods of linguistic philosophy. Such a
turn of events is undesirable enough in itself, but it has had the
further consequence of reducing philosophy to an internal dialogue among professionals so that even those in other disciplines
have been led to believe that the analytic approach is *the* voice
of philosophy and all other voices are old-fashioned, unscientif-
ic, or merely "metaphysical."

If philosophy is to recover itself in our time and acquire a
voice that will contribute something to the illumination and
resolution of contemporary human questions and concerns, it

will have to *reform* itself at at least three critical points: (1) It will have to take a more skeptical look at critical philosophy itself and come to see that the philosophical issues that we supposedly can discuss only *after* our tools and techniques have been set in order, *already arise* in that supposedly neutral preliminary; (2) It will have to abandon the subjunctive mood and approach the difficult questions directly, and not only in the terms set by asking how we *would* deal with such questions if we did, except that we do not; (3) It will have to recover a broader conception of experience and of reason, so that the former is no longer represented by droplets of sense, and the latter by formalized logic, for on such a basis the richness of experience is lost and such an empty reason is ill-equipped to deal with all the important issues of ethics, metaphysics, and religion.

VII

THE NEW NEED FOR A RECOVERY

OF PHILOSOPHY*

The first note to be struck concerns the underlying spirit of this occasion. I believe that Whitehead was profoundly right when he wrote in *Adventures of Ideas* that "philosophy is not—or at least, should not be—a ferocious debate between irritable professors."** Regardless of the undeniable differences in our points of view and approaches to philosophy, the present situation calls for a recovery of our subject in the form of a concerted attack upon problems arising from our efforts to define and sustain a life that is human as over against a war between philosophers largely bent on scoring points in an academic intelligence test. Several years ago during a meeting of this Association, I overheard a conversation between two junior members who had just come from attending a symposium. One said to the other, "What did you think of that? X shot down Y's paper and it was not altogether clear that he had read it!" If this is the essence of philosophy, then we should all disband!

I do not overlook the strife and rivalry that seems inevitable

*Presidential Address, American Philosophical Association, Eastern Division. 78th Annual Meeting, Philadelphia, Pennsylvania, December 27–30, 1981.
**Adventures of Ideas, New York: Macmillan, 1937, p. 125.

223

in every intellectual and professional field of endeavor, including the sciences as evidenced, to take but one example, by the claims of Leakey *vis-à-vis* those of other paleoanthropologists. And, at its best, discussion and debate over even the most fundamental differences can and does make a significant contribution to the attainment of knowledge and the avoidance of error. The fact remains, however, that for all the talk there has been among philosophers in recent decades about being "scientific," there has been far too little appreciation of the cooperative spirit to be found in the sciences where many inquirers working in concert and sharing results have accomplished what would perhaps elude any single individual. Schopenhauer says somewhere that philosophers invariably claim to be in pursuit of truth, but that it is remarkable how little of it they seem to find in the books of their colleagues. I am not unaware that the analogy between philosophy and the sciences is not exact nor that there is no precise counterpart in philosophical discussion for the experimental procedures in science where cooperation and the comparison of results is most evident. Neither am I disregarding the intense intramural discussions that have taken place in recent decades among philosophers who are in agreement about some basic position or way of approach. Too much of this discussion, however, has been insular and has militated against the admittedly difficult but also essential exchange between basically different outlooks and approaches. The unfortunate consequence has been an almost universal failure of anyone to learn from anyone else, or if anyone does, no one will admit it.

No better illustration of this state of affairs can be found than in the neglect, at least until very recently, on the part of many philosophers in America of the heritage of the pragmatists. It is important to notice that a number of telling points made by Rorty in his recent book, *Philosophy and the Mirror of Nature*, had been made by these thinkers decades ago. With the exception of James at some points, they all attacked what is now called foundationalism, rejected the priority of epistemology, denied to philosophy a certainty not to be found even in empirical science, never accepted the "given" even before it became a myth, and above all they were devoted to the need for philosophical conversation cutting across party lines.

The intriguing question is why did these insights remain unknown to a great majority of professional philosophers, or, if they were known, why were they neglected? Or is it perhaps the case that, once positions become solidified, one is able to learn only from the internal development taking place within the position one has adopted? If this is so, then from the standpoint of economy alone, considerable effort is wasted when we must discover on our own what we might have learned from others were the lines of communication more open. It seems to me that a major factor leading to the reduction in communication among philosophers has been the loss of a faith in reason as a synoptic, generalizing and unifying power. The more narrowly reason is conceived, the less possibility there is that we can achieve a comprehensive understanding of the interconnections between the many facets of experience articulated in the different philosophical standpoints that now exist. The shrinkage of reason in scope and power not only threatens mutual understanding, but it also has the adverse effect of driving the vaguer and less tractable philosophical problems beyond the range of rational criticism where they are appropriated by those who care little for scientific knowledge and have few scruples about rational consistency.

More than sixty years ago John Dewey wrote an essay about his diagnosis of the contemporary philosophical scene entitled, "The Need for a Recovery of Philosophy." It is from this essay that I adapt my title. There he made a plea for a return to a

direct approach to philosophical issues as they arise from conflicts and problematic situations encountered in the moral, social, political and scientific contexts of American culture. Dewey
pointed to the futility of philosophical preliminaries as represented by the continuing emphasis on the theory of knowledge,
a topic he viewed with suspicion not only because it served to
postpone the discussion of other important issues, but because
a problem of knowledge *überhaupt* he regarded as stemming
from a non-empirical conception of experience. Consequently,
Dewey devoted the bulk of his essay to a critique of classical
empiricism and the epistemology "industry" as he called it,
developing in place of both a new theory of experience more
conducive to the direct treatment of philosophical problems
which he advocated.

Unfortunately, Dewey's plea fell on deaf ears and, ironically
enough, the professional philosophy of the Anglo-American
tradition not only continued to focus on the theory of knowledge, on logic, semantics and language, but there was as well
a resurgence of the very empiricism that Dewey had attacked.
The development of American pragmatism that started with
the anti-Cartesian essays of Peirce in the 1860s and continued
through the work of James, Dewey and others was, for the
most part, set aside by philosophers who more and more came
to view themselves as engaged in a professional activity. The
tradition of Hume was reinstated through the powerful influence of Russell and Ayer especially and reenforced by the new
logic, a far more potent instrument than the association of
ideas. Perhaps the main reason for this reversal is to be found
in the embarrassment of many philosophers in the face of
science and the consequent attempts to make philosophy scientific. Whatever the reason, there remains the fact that too few
philosophers bothered to understand the new philosophical orientation marked out by the pragmatists because they were too

ready to accept the adverse criticism it received at the hands of Russell and others. In view of these developments and the fact that Dewey's plea for a recovery of a philosophy in touch with the problems of the culture went unheeded makes it necessary to advance that plea once again.

The decline of philosophy as an influential voice in the intellectual exchange within our culture has been the result of several questionable conceptions that have dominated much of modern philosophy since the seventeenth century. Not least among the consequences of this loss of an audible voice has been the migration to other fields of study of many questions upon which philosophers used to concentrate: the place of man in the cosmic order, the status of human purpose in a seemingly mechanical universe, the basic categories and modes of being, the problem of God, and what an ancient philosopher called "the things that matter most." We should not therefore be surprised to discover that literary critics, intellectual historians, novelists, psychiatrists, economists and those in the biological sciences, to name but a few, are capturing the imagination of the public through discussion of many philosophical issues and concerns. One might say that such a turn of events is not to be condemned outright, especially if one has doubts about whether philosophers should think of themselves as being in sole possession of a clearly defined intellectual territory. We have, moreover, to consider that the discussion of important questions is what really matters regardless of who carries it on. Upon second thought, it should be apparent that our present situation is not satisfactory and does not represent a stable solution. The requisite philosophical skill and insight required for treating reflective questions is often lacking in those who are unaware of what is to be learned from the heritage of philosophical thinking we possess.

Three beliefs have prevented philosophy from having its

proper impact: *first*, the belief in the possibility of attaining certainty or finality, whether in substance or approach; *secondly*, the belief that prior to the actual engagement with a philosophical issue it is necessary to put our intellectual apparatus in an agreed upon order; *thirdly*, the belief that philosophy can be made "scientific" by reducing it to those areas such as logic and the philosophy of science where it is thought that certifiable solutions are possible. These beliefs are well known and therefore do not call for any lengthy exposition; less emphasis, however, has been placed on the difficulties they have brought about, first by diverting philosophy from its main task of relating the inescapable abstractions of thought to each other and to our primary experience of the world, and secondly by turning philosophy into a specialty concerned with purely technical matters bearing no direct relation to the perplexities confronting human beings in a precarious world.

As regards certainty and the power it has exercised in modern philosophy, there are two important points to be made. The first is that the pursuit of certainty led to a loss of the concrete world encountered in ordinary experience and to the belief that philosophy, especially, has to do primarily with the contents of the mind. The second point is that the hankering after certainty by philosophers long after it had been abandoned as an ideal by science misled many into believing that we do not have to settle for a merely hypothetical, fallible and modifiable body of philosophical opinions, but can "do better" by appealing to foundations and necessary starting points. The loss of the concrete world came about as the result of reducing the object to the object of knowledge, to ideas in the mind, to sensible appearances; in short, to whatever philosophers thought one could be certain about, letting the world fall where it may. In the wake of this reduction, philosophy came to be regarded as having a privileged concern with the mind and with the problem of how the human mind could, as it were, leap over itself in order to reach an external world. The problem is, of course, insoluble as stated, but much effort has gone into discussing it which might have been more fruitfully expended.

On the matter of what I have called "doing better," the point I wish to make is that philosophers have sometimes alienated both their colleagues in other fields and the man on the street by assuming as air of intellectual superiority and refusing to rest content with the support of ordinary experience, common-sense and premises which we have no valid reason to doubt. Peirce, citing Hume's confession that he found his premises satisfactory, remarked, "he seems to be dissatisfied with himself for being satisfied." In philosophy we need not attempt to improve on the situation in which we can give reasons for our opinions and have no overriding reasons for doubting them.

The second belief which, in my view, has blocked the road to direct inquiry into first order philosophical questions is that before we can engage in such inquiry it is necessary to determine the capacity of our knowing apparatus, our language and our logic. This belief has taken numerous forms, but they all stem from the reflexive term initiated by Locke when he proposed to postpone discussion of questions on which philosophers disagree in order to assess the competence of our understanding for dealing with such questions. As Whitehead put it, the ancients asked, what do we know? and the moderns ask, how do we know? I have two comments to make concerning the perpetuation of the reflexive turn. First, as we can learn from the history of modern philosophy and the state of much contemporary philosophy, whatever preliminary investigations have been thought necessary before we can get to philosophy, themselves all involve philosophical considerations and serve only to shift the discussion from the drawing room to the vesti-

bule. Since, moreover, we never succeed in putting our epistemological house in order, the questions postponed in the process remain indefinitely postponed; all our energy is spent in
working our way to the starting line and the real philosophical
race never begins.

My second comment about the reflexive turn concerns the
inverted state of affairs it has brought about. Berkeley made
the point when, in defense of direct perception, he said that
we do not see with geometry. If I may paraphrase his remark,
I would say that we do not mean with a theory meaning, we do
not communicate with a theory of communication and we do
not know with epistemology. Whatever be the role and place of
such theories, they must not be allowed to come first as constituting the entrance requirements for philosophical thinking,
for, if they do, the charade of postponement will be reenacted.
We need constantly to remind ourselves that before philosophy
can become critical there must be on the ground some philosophical opinion to be criticized. And, in any case, criticism
cannot be a matter of judging positions in accordance with abstract and formal criteria, since the adequacy and elucidatory
power of any set of ideas can be judged only when they are
at work actually articulating the subject matter. Critical thinking must be about results, not roots.

The third belief that has had its effect in emptying philosophy concerns the many attempts to turn it into something scientific by reducing its scope to those tools and topics where it is
supposed that genuine progress and certified results can be
achieved. This belief, it seems to me, is not now as pervasive
as it once was, but it has been very influential in diverting
many philosophers from the discussion of speculative questions
which are especially difficult and recalcitrant because, among
other reasons, their very formulation involves us in metaphysical assumptions that are open to debate. I believe, however,

that at present philosophers have less need to be embarrassed, as they were some decades ago, in the face of adverse comparisons between a steadily progressive science and philosophy seen as no more than a jumble of conflicting opinions. Studies in the history of science have served to alter the picture; not only has the line between science and philosophy become indistinct by the questioning of the steady progress thesis in science, but also there is a new understanding of the open-endedness of the sciences and an acknowledgment of the existence of more than one school of thought on many scientific issues, so that differences of opinion can no longer be regarded as the exclusive possession of philosophers.

Against this background, I should now like to offer some specific conditions, the fulfillment of which would, in my view, contribute greatly to the recovery of philosophy as a significant force in American society. These conditions can be taken as defining the shape of philosophy in that comprehensive sense manifested in the thought of the great philosophical minds from which all of us have continued to derive insight and inspiration whether we agree with them or not. I have four conditions and four consequent aims in mind. There is *first*, the need for philosophy to root itself in the crude experience we all undergo or live through which comes to be preserved in language, social institutions and in the various forms of human activity that make up the common life of a people. From this crude experience there springs a body of beliefs and expectations forming a fund of commonsense serving as a base for philosophical interpretation. *Secondly*, we must set aside the belief, derived largely from the image of building an edifice, that philosophy must have a privileged starting point which somehow is to serve as a support for whatever is supposed to follow from it. This approach limits philosophy to the selective bias of the starting point and is thus bound to exclude a large range of experience. *Thirdly,* we must reconsider the peculiar nature of philosophy as being neither a special science, on the one hand, nor the work of esthetic imagination, on the other, and resist the temptation to turn philosophy into a professional specialty dominated by a technical vocabulary. *Finally,* we must cease thinking of critical assessment in philosophy solely as a matter of the success with which a certain program is carried out without regard to interaction with other positions. Instead, we must return to a dialectical conception wherein we attempt to make critical comparisons between alternative positions for the purpose of determining how illuminating, comprehensive and coherent a given position proves to be when it is *at work* interpreting the world. In no other way can conversation among philosophers be recovered on a broad scale.

I have done no more than state these conditions in a preliminary way; let me now attempt to explain what they mean in more detail. To say that philosophy must find a base in crude experience is to insist on the priority of experience as we live through or undergo it. Such experience is always a part of a personal biography wherein the individual gropes for some understanding of what the experience means and how it "fits into" a larger life pattern. Experience in this sense, as Heidegger, Bergson, James and others have pointed out, is not the same as the objectified experience of the theoretical observer taking note of data that are the same for everyone. In lived experience the self does not merely look at what it lives through, but is aware of being engaged in it and constituted by it. This is not to say that a sound philosophy can ignore what we know of ourselves and the world in the form of objectified experience. It is to say that the latter, couched as it must be in a standard form and in technical language, cannot be the base from which philosophy sets out. To illustrate the point, I borrow an example from Lionel Trilling. Out of our lived experience we say, "We fell in love and married," but if this experience were to be objectified, we would find ourselves having to say, "Their libidinal impulses being reciprocal, they integrated their individual erotic drives and brought them within the same frame of reference."* This conceptualized, reflected product is not an articulation of, nor does it evoke, the lived experience from which reflective thought must take its rise in an effort to plumb the meaning of human love and the hopes, fears, joys and sorrows of the marital relation.

Just as objectifying experience may serve to obscure experience as actually undergone, an overemphasis on expression, both word and concept, may have the same effect. Consider, for example, the tendency in which we all share to some degree when confronting a philosophical problem to focus attention first on a concept or a term. If the problem has to do with freedom, for example, our initial focus should be on *situations*, actual or imagined, in which deliberation, choice, decision and action are all involved. Starting instead with a meaning fixed by the term "freedom," we are likely to be diverted from attending to the relevant human situations in which the problem of freedom is to be understood. One consequence is that this problem then becomes one of theory alone—a philosopher's problem—and we lose sight of the fact that everyone confronts it all the time in lived experience. The point is of the utmost importance, for when philosophical problems are not perceived in the conflicts and dilemmas in thought and action which confront everyone, they are bound to appear as occasioned only by what philosophers themselves say and therefore as the exclusive concern of professionals. No one of the major philosophers from whom we have learned the most envisaged themselves as dealing exclusively with a set of pre-packaged issues

---

*Lionel Trilling, "Contemporary American Literature in Its Relation to Ideas," *American Quarterly*, Vol. I., Number 3 (Fall, 1949), p. 198. I am indebted to Dr. Jo Ann Boydston, Director, The Center for Dewey Studies, Southern Illinois University for locating this citation.

passed on by their predecessors. Each philosophized in response to their special interest in understanding some basic
features of the world which might then offer clues to the interpretation of the rest of experience. Aristotle's thought was determined throughout by his attempt to grasp the structure of
living things; Plato's was shaped by his response to the dilemmas of ethics and politics and their bearing on the good life;
Whitehead's by the concern to relate the well-founded abstractions of science to the continuum of living experience. In every
case it was the nature of the world and the perplexities of individual and social life that gave rise to philosophical thinking.

No philosophy can afford to ignore the offshoot of lived experience that becomes solidified in the form of commonsense.
Berkeley, it will be recalled, thought it not only odd but detrimental that philosophers should invariably turn out to be
in doubt about so many matters which the plain man believes
on the basis of pervasive and uncontradicted experience.
Berkeley's concern was that "the mob" would cease believing
anything philosophers might say in virtue of their seemingly
infinite capacity to doubt everything. A due respect for commonsense does not, however, require that we accept it without
reflective criticism and questioning. Here philosophers are
called upon to clear up the vagueness of the language in which
commonsense finds expression, and to seek to reconcile its
paradoxes and inconsistencies without losing the core of truth
that is in it, a core resting on a fund of experience far greater
than that possessed by any individual. Commonsense is not un-
assailable by doubt, but it should be doubted only for specific
reasons that point us to the difficulty to be resolved. Wholesale skepticism is often fruitless because its exponents fail to
take responsibility for a solution, being content to detect the
errors in the solutions of others.

The second condition has to do with overcoming the belief
that there are privileged starting points in philosophy, whether

in the form of particular elements such as the data of the senses, or special enterprises such as the theory of knowledge or of meaning. Peirce was right in objecting to the injuction that reflective thought must begin at this point or that with the claim that no one can begin at any point other than where they actually are. If we attend to the facts about how we think as philosophers we find that we always begin in the middle of things with a set of inherited beliefs made up of funded experience and we take these beliefs to be settled until they are challenged by novel experience, specific doubts and the entertainment of hitherto unthought of possibilities. In short, the matrix of philosophical thinking is one in which we are never actually in doubt about every belief nor are we ever in possession of certainty about any belief. That is the fluid and potentially creative situation in which we exist and all attempts to improve upon it by introducing incorrigible first principles or the like can only be self-deceptive.

Since no thought, philosophical or otherwise, proceeds without assumptions, it is imperative that a candid disclosure of these assumptions be made at the outset. An open display of the cards with which we intend to play not only enables others to understand better what we are trying to say, but it forestalls fruitless controversy engendered by those who would have us believe that they play with no cards at all. Proceeding in the daylight, moreover, frees us from the need to make *antecedent* claims for the rightness, superiority or necessity of these assumptions since they will be weighed in the balance of the consequences that follow from putting them to work in the actual interpretation of the world and human life. Only in this way can we hope to assess the explanatory power of any set of philosophical assumptions. The focus of attention, in addition, is shifted from the preliminary consideration of entrance requirements to the eventual appraisal of the adequacy of results. And in fact such an approach is the only one that assures us that there will be any results at all, since philosophical skirmishes over the entrance requirements for philosophical thought are always inconclusive; they postpone, through fatigue or distraction, all efforts to achieve constructive results. If we were to liken the philosophical enterprise to the adventure of going into a theater, it is time that we gave more consideration to the possibility that having a ticket to get in is less important than having to show one to get out!

The third condition calls for reconsideration of the peculiar character of philosophy as neither a special science nor an expression of the esthetic imagination represented by the novelist or poet. The issue bearing most closely on our loss of communication beyond the professional and academic circle concerns how we are to carry out the tasks of criticism and interpretation so as not to lose all contact with the language through which members of our society regularly communicate. Perhaps some light can be thrown on the problem by considering philosophy in relation to the sciences, on the one hand, and to creative literature, on the other.

To begin with, the theoretical aims determining, for example, the study of planetary systems or the origins of hominid existence require the development of technical language encompassing a degree of detail and precision of meaning far exceeding that required for purposes of ordinary experience and communication. The disparity between the two forms of expression is accepted as something dictated by the different purposes involved. Except when scientists set out to explain their theories for the benefit of laymen—as seems to be happening more and more—they are under no constraint to describe and explain their basic research in the terms that suffice for conducting our daily affairs.

On the other hand, if we consider the domain of creative literature, the situation appears quite different. The ordinary means of communication and the funded experience of a culture constitute a stable background not to be ignored by the creative writer. This holds true even when Joyce, Emily Dickenson or Ezra Pound transform familiar language and reshape experience in ways that may elude anyone totally caught in the web of ordinary words and conventional experience. There is, however, no counterpart in the world of literature for the technical languages of the sciences. The writer seeking to evoke the haunting sense of a moor illuminated intermittently by the moon's success in eluding a floating cloud, will certainly not need to give a geological account of the moor, nor an explanation of the moon's phases. The author will avail himself instead of lived experience for his effect, enhanced by an imaginative skill in expression which depends on the resources inherent in the language of the reader's community.

The vexing problem we as philosophers face at this point stems from the fact that reflective thinking does not fit into the linguistic pattern of either science or imaginative literature. We cannot opt for a purely technical language as our means of expression because the matters we discuss are of concern to everyone, and to sever all connections with familiar discourse means failure to reach anyone other than professional philosophers. And, I should add, this failure of communication does not stop with the ordinary reader or man in the street. Some years ago I was asked to give a talk to the English Institute at Columbia about philosophy and literature. In the ensuing discussion, Marjorie Hope Nicholson, scarcely an ordinary reader, asked why she could no longer understand much that modern philosophers write, prefacing her question with the comment that this was not at all the case in her student days earlier on in the century. The heavy task laid upon us, then, is to plumb the resources inherent in the basic language of the culture in an effort to refine and reshape it for our purposes. This does not mean claiming that we can speak of objects and persons, unity and identity, being and process, possibility and necessity solely in terms of the discourse that functions successfully in post offices, department stores and railway stations. It is rather that we cannot turn our backs on the language of the culture if we wish to be understood by anyone but ourselves. As Brand Blanshard has pointed out in his incisive little book, *On Philosophical Style*, the ultimate challenge to a philosopher is to develop the style in which to convey substantial philosophical opinions so that a non-specialist will not give up after the first page. Howsoever we come to terms with the language of the culture, it seems clear that, in an age of science and technology especially, we cannot achieve the aims of philosophical reflection through the medium of poetic or imaginative expression.

The dilemma of communication is well illustrated in the contrast between the styles of James and Whitehead. James was not primarily engaged in analyzing ordinary language, but rather in *using* it to express philosophical opinions, some of which were quite out of the ordinary. The advantages James gained by writing and speaking in pungent and often colloquial language were often offset by subsequent misunderstandings. Consider James' attempts to make pragmatism clear and straightforward by making such statements as "the true is the expedient in the way of knowing," or the true belief is the one that is "satisfactory" and the true idea is the one that "works." It should be obvious that terms like these drawn from ordinary discourse required some philosophical dry-cleaning if they were to express the main ideas of pragmatism with a minimum of ambiguity.

At the opposite extreme, Whitehead opted for a formidable, philosophical terminology that made no claim to continuity with the language used in other situations and contexts. His choice was dictated by the aim of avoiding language connoting a substance/attribute view of things in order to set forth the philosophy of organism according to which the ultimate constituents of reality are events. Consequently, he had recourse to "prehension," "actual occasions," "concrescences" and the like, terms that have indeed become familiar within a circle of specialists, but it is unlikely that any of these terms will make their way into ordinary speech.

What lessons are to be learned from the foregoing comparison? It seems to me that there are three such lessons. The first and most obvious is that there are difficulties in both approaches and hence that neither one can be taken as an ideal model. While the use of colloquial expressions seems to bring philosophy down from the clouds and within the reach of everyone, the vagueness and ambiguity attaching to such expressions easily lead to misunderstanding which, in turn, needs to be overcome by further clarification. Unfortunately, this cannot always be accomplished because the colloquialisms stick and the clarification is sometimes ignored. On the other hand, excessive use of technical terms and especially neologisms makes communication on a broad scale virtually impossible, since the meaning of these expressions needs to be explained even to other professionals.

Secondly, in my view, the refinement of the language on hand offers better prospects for communication than does the introduction of novel terminology. Hence, I suggest that we focus less on the disparity between ordinary forms of expression and technical language and more on the distinction between *vagueness* and *precision*, a distinction cutting across all discourse. No expression in successful use is totally vague and no expression is so precise that it could not, for certain purposes, be made more so. Let us take an example. Suppose we show a person unacquainted with mathematics a nicely constructed Möbius strip and a simple ring collar and ask for a comparison between the two. There is nothing wrong with a person saying from direct observation and commonsense that one has a "twist" in it and looks like a pretzel, whereas the other is "round" and looks like a doughnut. The answer, however, is extremely vague and stands in the need of refinement, something we can accomplish by saying that one of the figures has but one side and one edge, whereas the other has two sides and two edges. We have thus moved from a vague expression to one that is more precise and without the introduction of any technical terms. Taking a cue from this example, I suggest that if, as philosophers, we saw ourselves not as practitioners of a specialty with a technical language, but as reflective thinkers seeking to describe, interpret and illuminate lived experience by making more precise the vague expressions of ordinary communication, we would more successfully fulfill our function and still retain a voice in the intellectual dialogue of the culture.

The fourth and last condition can be expressed briefly since it has already been mentioned. Philosophy is not the sort of enterprise where we can achieve verification in any strict sense. We need not, however, conclude that no critical assessment among philosophical positions is possible at all. If we were to estimate the adequacy and viability of any philosophy by comparing its elucidatory power with that of other alternatives, the result would be just the dialectical exchange needed to recover our subject. This approach, I contend, is more fruitful than assessing a position solely with respect to the success with which it carries out a program totally unrelated to other alternatives. As Hegel showed so well, any philosophical position can, in principle, do justice to that region of experience or dimension of things selected as a focus of attention. But what of the capacity of the position to account for what it omits? A philosophical demand for comprehensiveness and coherence is thrust upon us and it must be imposed as a touchstone for any system of thought. If, however, philosophical construction is confined to what I have called program philosophy, no dialectical exchange ever takes place because programs are strictly intramural affairs. This point was impressed upon me years ago by an invitation to participate in a symposium that was part of an Inter-American Congress of Philosophy; the topic was "Nominalism." Not then knowing the rules, I assumed that this was to be a discussion of the strengths and weaknesses of some more or less agreed upon philosophical position going by that name. As it turned out, I was quite mistaken; with but one exception, the other participants simply assumed that nominalism was correct so that the only remaining problem was how to state the position in the clearest and most consistent way. Any questioning of that assumption was regarded as inappropriate. In my view, this sort of thing is not philosophical dialogue.

In concluding this address, I cannot pass over the paradoxical note it must strike. I have criticized the postponement of substantive philosophical discussion coming as the result of preoccupation with preliminaries and yet it would appear that I have been an accomplice to the error of speaking almost entirely *about* philosophy. The topic, however, is unavoidable at a time when the question of the nature and role of philosophy has itself become a substantive issue. Given the nature of the subject to which we are all devoted, I would not expect us to agree about what constitutes such a protean undertaking and how it is to be pursued. I am, however, quite sure that we shall make little progress in discussing the matter if we start with the misguided assumption that there are but *two* contending approaches and outlooks involved. The plain truth is that there are many more alternatives than that; the task before us now is to initiate a serious dialogue among the many different philosophical opinions represented in this Association. I believe that this can happen only if everyone is prepared to abandon two claims; first, that any single approach to philosophy is the only legitimate one, and secondly, that those pursuing philosophical inquiry in any fashion other than one's own are *ipso facto* not engaged in philosophy at all. The first of these claims concerns respect for philosophy and the second respect for persons. If we do not convey the impression of being earnestly in pursuit of the truth, of trying to find out what there is and where we fit into the scheme of things, we must not expect our readers and hearers to be either interested or moved. In short, if we do not believe each other, no one else will believe us. If we can recover among ourselves the sense that the baffling character of philosophical problems demands nothing less than a cooperative endeavor instead of partisan strife, we shall have taken an important step forward in the direction of recovering for philosophy itself a more powerful and respected voice in our culture.

BIBLIOGRAPHICAL NOTE

The philosophers whose ideas we have discussed were all pro-
lific writers. Their collected works, consisting of books, essays,
addresses, lectures, and reviews, would fill many shelves. In
every case the principal writings are well known and have been
widely circulated. Some new material has come to light in recent years and older works, long out of print, have again become available. Unfortunately, however, many important works
have been neglected and interpreters have formed opinions
that leave them out of account.

In reading Peirce it is important not to lose sight of the basically metaphysical drift of his thought. He constantly drove back
to ultimate questions. The standard works are found in *Collected Papers of Charles Sanders Peirce*, Vols. I–VI, edited by
Charles Hartshorne and Paul Weiss, Cambridge, 1931–35. Recently two volumes, VII and VIII (1958), have been added to
this set under the editorship of Arthur W. Burks. The reader is
directed to Volume VIII, 251 ff., for a bibliography of Peirce's
writings along with reference to previous bibliographical lists.
Attention is also called to *Charles S. Peirce's Letters to Lady
Welby*, edited by Irwin C. Lieb, New Haven, 1953. These letters
deal with the theory of meaning and the classification of signs.
Volume VI of the *Collected Papers* remains as the chief source
of Peirce's metaphysical and religious ideas.

243

All of James's works have been widely circulated and many are available in translation. A more balanced picture of James would have resulted if less attention had been paid to such essays as "The Will To Believe" and more to his radical empiricism. The pragmatism associated with the name of James does not exhaust his thought; the essays contained in *Essays in Radical Empiricism* express his distinctive theory of experience and his attempt to construe reality as "a world of pure experience." The connection between James's descriptive psychology and the phenomenological standpoint of Husserl becomes ever more clear; in this regard see J. Linschoten, *Auf dem Weg zu einer phänomenologischen Psychologie*, Berlin, 1961.

It would be difficult to find a parallel in philosophical interpretation to the one-sided fashion in which Dewey's philosophy has been treated by his allies and critics alike. His views on education, school, society, and science have often been taken as the whole of his thought. Important as were (and are) such works as *How We Think*, Boston, 1910, *Democracy and Education*, New York, 1916, and *Human Nature and Conduct*, New York, 1922, they must not be allowed to overshadow *Experience and Nature*, Chicago and London, 1925, the most fully elaborated naturalistic metaphysic in American thought. Of further importance for his philosophical position are such papers as "The Need for a Recovery of Philosophy" and "The Postulate of Immediate Empiricism." See the excellent collection of papers by Richard J. Bernstein, *On Experience, Nature and Freedom*, New York, 1960. The most complete bibliography of Dewey's writings is found in *The Philosophy of John Dewey*, edited by Paul Arthur Schilpp, 2nd ed., New York, 1951.

Exclusive concentration on Royce's argument for the Absolute Knower in *The Religious Aspect of Philosophy*, Boston, 1885, has resulted in the failure to understand the voluntaristic aspect of his thought and his aim of synthesizing intellect and will. Further attention to the Fourth Conception of Being in

The World and the Individual, 2 vols., New York, 1900–1901, will correct one-sided impressions. The use of Peirce's theory of interpretation in *The Problem of Christianity,* 2 vols., New York, 1913, shows Royce's interest in the problem of religious meaning long before it became a central topic for analytic philosophy. I have analyzed the theory of interpretation and community in *Royce's Social Infinite,* New York, 1950. For a list of Royce's books and articles consult J. H. Cotton, *Royce on the Human Self,* Cambridge, 1954, 305ff., and *Royce's Social Infinite,* 171–3.

Whitehead's writings have circulated widely. Since his works vary in complexity and difficulty, not all could be expected to have the same influence. Curiously enough, works less difficult to comprehend than *Process and Reality,* New York, 1929, have not received all the attention they deserve. Among neglected books are *Religion in the Making,* New York, 1926, *The Function of Reason,* Princeton, 1929, *Adventures of Ideas,* New York, 1933. The most complete bibliography of Whitehead's writings is found in *The Philosophy of Alfred North Whitehead,* edited by Paul Arthur Schilpp, Evanston and Chicago, 1941.

There are indications at present of original philosophical thinking that is directed toward the solution of fundamental issues. In these works will be found the best clues to the future of constructive philosophy on the American scene. F. S. C. Northrop made a pioneering effort in his *Meeting of East and West,* New York, 1946, aimed at understanding basic differences in philosophical perspective between Western culture and the Oriental world. He has dealt in a provocative way with problems arising out of the impact of science on the arts and humanistic studies in *The Logic of the Sciences and the Humanities,* New York, 1947, and, more recently, with the problems of ethics and legal philosophy in *The Complexity of Legal and Ethical Experience,* Boston, 1959.

J. H. Randall, Jr., makes a fresh approach to the history of philosophy in *The Career of Philosophy,* New York, 1962. He aims at showing the importance of historical treatment for constructive philosophical thinking. In addition he carries on the naturalistic tradition of Dewey, Santayana, and Woodbridge in his *Nature and Historical Experience*, New York, 1958.

Paul Weiss's *Modes of Being*, Carbondale, 1958, is the most original piece of speculative philosophy to appear for many decades. Dealing with the inescapable problem of the one and the many, he offers an original theory according to which the meaning of Being is found in a certain type of togetherness of four modes of Being. Weiss is one of the few philosophers at present who establishes connections with theological thought; his treatment of God as a mode of Being is noteworthy.

The typically American openness to philosophical ideas of a novel and creative sort is well exemplified in John Wild's recent studies in the fields of Phenomenology and Existential philosophy. His *Challenge of Existentialism*, Bloomington, 1955, represents a clear-headed account of the meaning of the philosophy of existence for the present philosophical situation. His book, *Human Freedom and Social Order*, Durham, 1959, explores the idea of a Christian philosophy with special attention to the issues of ethics.

Charles Hartshorne's recent book, *The Logic of Perfection*, LaSalle, 1962, contains in its title essay the most complete analysis of the logical basis for the ontological argument that has ever been given. In other essays he carries forward the "neoclassical" or "panentheistic" interpretation of God introduced in earlier works, *The Divine Relativity*, New Haven, 1948, and *Man's Vision of God*, Chicago, 1937.

The work of W. V. Quine brings to a focus the bearing of formal and second-intentional considerations on substantive philosophical issues. In addition to writings in mathematical logic, we may cite *From a Logical Point of View*, Cambridge, 1953, and *Word and Object*, Cambridge, 1960.

In the almost two decades since this book first appeared many important contributions to the literature concerning the thinkers here represented have been made. The following short list is a selection with emphasis falling on comprehensive interpretations rather than treatments of individual thinkers.

Ayer, Sir Alfred J. *The Origins of Pragmatism.* San Francisco, 1968.

Boller, Paul F. *Freedom and Fate in American Thought From Edwards to Dewey.* Dallas, 1978.

Caws, Peter, Ed. *Two Centuries of Philosophy in America.* Oxford, 1980.

Eames, S. M. *Pragmatic Naturalism.* Carbondale, 1977.

Flower, Elizabeth and Murphey, Murray. *A History of Philosophy in America.* 2 vols. New York, 1977.

Gavin, W. M. and Blakely, T. J. *Russia and America; a Philosophical Comparison.* Dordrecht, 1976.

Kuklick, Bruce. *The Rise of American Philosophy.* New Haven, 1977.

McDermott, John. *The Culture of Experience.* New York, 1976.

Reck, Andrew J. *Recent American Philosophy.* New York, 1964.

——. *The New American Philosophers.* Baton Rouge, 1968.

Roth, Robert J. *American Religious Philosophy.* New York, 1967.

Schneider, Herbert W. *A History of American Philosophy.* 2nd ed. New York, 1963.

Sellars, Roy Wood. *Reflections on American Philosophy from Within.* Notre Dame, 1969.

Smith, John E., Ed. *Contemporary American Philosophy.* Second Series. London and New York, 1970.

————. *Purpose and Thought; the Meaning of Pragmatism.* London and New Haven, 1978.

Thayer, H. S. *Meaning and Action; A Study of American Pragmatism.* Indianapolis and New York, 1973.

White, Morton. *Pragmatism and the American Mind.* New York, 1973.

Wilshire, Bruce. *William James and Phenomenology.* Bloomington, 1968.

In addition to these interpretations of the development of philosophy in America, new editions of the classical philosophers are now forthcoming. The comprehensive edition, *The Collected Works of John Dewey*, under the General Editorship of Jo Ann Boydston who is also Director of the Center for Dewey Studies at Southern Illinois University, has thus far made available Dewey's works up to 1925, including a new edition of *Experience and Nature*. An *Edition of the Works of William James*, under the Editorship of Dr. Frederick H. Burkhardt, is also well under way; thus far eight volumes have been published and the remaining volumes are now being prepared. A new twenty volume edition of the writings of Charles Sanders Peirce is also in progress under the Editorship of Professor Max H. Fisch and the first volume is to appear in the spring of 1982. Peirce's writings will be presented in chronological order, starting with those of 1857.

INDEX

Absolute, the, 81, 86, 91f., 98, 100, 106, 115, 190; absolutism, 86, 89
abstraction, 164 f., 171 ff., 179 ff., 183 f., 216, 234
action, 58 ff., 66 ff., 70, 72 ff., 76, 87, 98 ff., 128ff., 134 ff., 145, 147, 154, 168, 188, 192, 194 f., 213 f.; course of, 130 ff., 147 f., 155, 193
activity, *see* action
adaptation, 63 ff.
adjustment, 88 ff., 189
aesthetic experience, *see* art
Agapasm, 33
Agapasticism, 6, 32
Agassiz, Louis, 161
Aquinas, 221
Aristotle, 47, 82, 117, 139, 234
Arnold, Matthew, 109
art, 157 f., 169, 194, 197, 202, 208
assumption, 166 ff., 235
atomism, 169
atonement, 109, 194
Augustine, 112
authority, 101, 103, 207
Ayer, Sir Alfred J., 226, 247

Bacon, Francis, 51, 128, 167
Barzun, J., 32

belief, 9, 11 ff., 17 f., 22, 70, 76, 87 f., 114, 123, 188, 190, 194 f.
Bergson, H., 175, 211, 232
Berkeley, Bishop, 230, 234
biological approach, 117 ff., 127
Blakeley, T. J., 247
Blanshard, Brand, 238
Boller, Paul F., 247
Buddha, 70

Calvinism, 98
categories, 165 f., 173
causal connection, 49 f., 61, 67, 173, 221
causality, *see* causal connection
Caws, Peter, 247
Chance, 36
choice, 58, 71, 129, 138, 145, 154
Christ, 109, 111
Christianity, 34, 76, 98, 107 f., 111 f.
church, 110 ff.
civilization, 68 f., 160, 163 ff., 169, 173, 185, 188
collectivism, 84
community, 27 ff., 30, 65, 84, 90 ff., 95 f., 99 ff., 103, 105, 107, 109 f., 150, 163, 185, 190, 199, 205
Community, Beloved, 100 ff., 108 ff.

249